111 AI ChatGPT Transformative Prompts for Leadership Development & Maximum Potential

111 AI ChatGPT Transformative Prompts for Leadership Development & Maximum Potential

Attain Leadership Success with High-Impact, Low-Effort Strategies. Prompts Fit for ChatGPT, Copilot, Gemini & Llama

Mindscape Artwork Publishing
Mauricio Vasquez

Toronto, Canada

Authors:
Mauricio Vasquez

First Printing: November 2023

ISBN-978-1-990709-86-9 (Paperback)

ISBN-978-1-998402-13-7 (Hardcover)

DEDICATION

To all professionals and aspiring leaders committed to advancing their careers and enriching their leadership skills: May this book serve as a valuable resource, equipping you with the insights and strategies to navigate the complexities of today's dynamic workplace.

INTRODUCTION

Welcome to a comprehensive guide that merges established practices in mentoring, coaching, and leadership with the transformative power of Generative Artificial Intelligence (AI). Authored by Mauricio Vasquez, an expert in coaching and leadership, and AI-driven strategies, this book serves as a resource for professionals seeking to make a substantial impact in their field.

The current professional landscape demands agility, innovation, and significant influence. This book provides actionable insights to meet these challenges, enabled by Generative AI. The focus is not just on effective practices but on creating meaningful and measurable outcomes. The integration of Generative AI into professional development is more than a novelty; it's a necessity. This book tailors guidance, inspires strategies and facilitates highly effective professional interactions.

The objective is straightforward: to elevate your professional capabilities. Whether you're new to the workforce, an experienced leader, or someone looking to innovate, you'll find this book practical and enriching.

In essence, the book doesn't just introduce you to a toolkit; it aims to redefine your approach to professional leadership and interpersonal influence. Expect to delve into crafting effective interactions with others and optimized AI prompts, and to understand the dynamics of impactful leadership.

Let's begin the process of achieving enhanced professional effectiveness and influence. Welcome to your next steps in creating a meaningful, long-term impact.

ABOUT THE AUTHOR

Mauricio Vasquez is a multifaceted professional with over 20 years of experience in risk management and insurance, specializing in sectors like mining, power, and renewable energy. He holds an Industrial Engineering degree, a Master's in Business Administration, and a Master's in Marketing and Commercial Management, along with certifications in Enterprise Risk Management and Artificial Intelligence.

Mauricio is also a certified Adler Trained Coach and a self-published author, focusing on personal growth and professional development. His expertise in Artificial Intelligence and Large Language Models Prompt engineering adds a unique layer to his professional background. Fluent in both English and Spanish, Mauricio has worked across Canada, the U.S., Latin America, and the Caribbean. In addition to his corporate roles, he is a Professional and Life Coach, committed to helping immigrants transition successfully to new lives in Canada. His approach is deeply rooted in building long-term relationships and providing tailored, impactful solutions to clients.

If you want to connect with Mauricio, go to this link
https://www.linkedin.com/in/mauriciovasquez or scan this QR code:

7

WHAT IS GENERATIVE ARTIFICIAL INTELLIGENCE (AI)?

Within the transformative world of Artificial Intelligence (AI), Generative AI emerges as a paradigm-altering innovation. This is not merely an evolutionary step in data analytics; it's artificial intelligence capable of generating text, images, or other media, using generative models.

Generative AI takes a pioneering leap by producing original, value-driven content. Whether it's devising compelling emails, formulating tactical blueprints, or scripting empowering coaching dialogues, Generative AI not only enhances human potential but also ignites fresh avenues for personal and professional transformation.

This groundbreaking capacity is anchored in intricate neural network architectures adeptly trained to capture, replicate, and advance human-like behavioral patterns. The ramifications are profound and all-encompassing, impacting sectors as varied as marketing strategy, executive leadership, and personal development, to name just a few.

As we segue into our subsequent chapter focused on Natural Language Processing (NLP) Chatbots, understand that Generative AI acts as the foundational engine for these advanced interfaces. Specifically, within the frameworks of coaching, mentoring, and transformative leadership, Generative AI empowers these chatbots to conduct conversations that are not merely topical but deeply contextual and emotionally resonant. In doing so, it enriches the coaching experience, supplementing traditional methods with nuanced insights that are as data-informed as they are authentically human.

WHAT ARE NATURAL LANGUAGE PROCESSING CHATBOTS?

An Artificial Intelligence (AI) Chatbot is a program within a website or app that uses machine learning (ML) and natural language processing (NLP) to interpret inputs and understand the intent behind a request or "prompt" (more on this later in the book). Chatbots can be rule-based with simple use cases or more advanced and able to handle multiple conversations.

The rise of language models like GPT has revolutionized the landscape of conversational AI. These Chatbots now boast advanced capabilities that can mimic not just a human conversation style but also a (super) human mind. They can find information online and produce unique content and insights.

The most important thing to know about an AI Chatbot is that it combines ML and NLP to understand what people need and bring the best answers. Some AI Chatbots are better for personal use, like conducting research, and others are best for business use, like featuring a Chatbot on your company's website.

With this in mind, we've compiled a list of the best AI Chatbots at the time of the writing of this book. We strongly suggest that you try and test each of the most popular ones and see what works best for you.

ChatGPT:

- Uses NLP to understand the context of conversations to provide related and original responses in a human-like conversation.
- Multiple use cases for things like answering questions, ideating and getting inspiration, or generating new content [like a marketing email].
- Improves over time as it has more conversations.

Microsoft Copilot/Bing Chat:

- Uses NLP and ML to understand conversation prompts.
- The compose feature can generate original written content and images, and its powerful search engine capabilities can surface answers from the web.
- It's a conversational tool, so you can continue sending messages until you're satisfied.

Google Gemini/Bard:

- Google's Bard is a multi-use AI Chatbot.
- It's powered by Google's LaMDA [instead of GPT].
- Use it for things like brainstorming and ideation, drafting unique and original content, or getting answers to your questions.
- Connected to Google's website index so it can access information from the internet.

Meta LLaMa:

- Meta's Chatbot is an open source large language [LLM].
- The tool is trained using reinforcement learning from human feedback [RLHF], learning from the preferences and ratings of human AI trainers.

Starting from now, we will refer to these platforms as Chatbots. For a guide on how to sign up to each, please refer to Appendix No 1.

If you're seeking a beginner-friendly, step-by-step guide to using ChatGPT, please refer to Appendix No. 3. This appendix includes access to our report, "Elevate Your Productivity Using ChatGPT," which offers a detailed guide on leveraging ChatGPT to boost efficiency and productivity across a range of professional environments.

As of the book's publication date, the information herein is current and accurate. The Chatbot industry, however, is dynamic, with constant updates and new entrants. While specifics may evolve, our prompts, core strategies and principles discussed in this book are designed to withstand the test of time, offering you a robust framework for navigating this fast-paced landscape.

THE BENEFITS OF USING AI CHATBOTS IN YOUR COACHING, MENTORING AND LEADERSHIP JOURNEY

In today's rapidly evolving business landscape, the pursuit of effective leadership, coaching, and mentorship resembles a full-time commitment. Traditional approaches often require significant time and resources, but the advent of Chatbots and advanced conversational platforms like ChatGPT is a game-changer.

These AI-driven tools are becoming invaluable assets for professional development. They offer real-time coaching, behavioral insights, and actionable strategies, which can be applied by anyone aiming to climb the corporate ladder or make an impact as a leader.

The advantages of integrating Chatbots and the insights from this book into your leadership journey can be broken down into five key areas:

1. **Efficiency:** Chatbots can offer rapid, on-the-fly guidance that can dramatically expedite your leadership development cycle. They can help you formulate strategies, prepare for difficult conversations, or even fine-tune your leadership philosophy.
2. **Quality:** While the advice or strategies generated by Chatbots won't be perfect, they provide a solid starting point. By issuing clear and specific prompts, you can get actionable advice that can be fine-tuned to meet your unique leadership challenges.
3. **Edge:** In leadership, the ability to personalize your approach can be a unique advantage. Chatbots enable this level of personalization at scale. This allows you to adapt your leadership style and strategies to suit the distinct characteristics and needs of your team or organization, thereby standing out as a responsive leader.
4. **Innovative Insights:** Beyond standard guidance, Chatbots can be a springboard for creative thought. With the right prompts, you can unlock best practices and innovative leadership strategies that you can apply in your own unique context.
5. **Enhanced Self-Awareness:** This book is designed to be a robust tool to empower you in leadership and coaching roles. Coupled with Chatbots, you gain a more personalized form of guidance that can validate your skills and ambitions, boosting your confidence and equipping you to face a variety of leadership challenges.

By skillfully combining Chatbots with the actionable insights and strategies provided through this book, you're setting the stage for a potent blend of traditional wisdom and state-of-the-art technology. This fusion is set to redefine the frameworks of leadership, coaching, and mentorship in today's complex corporate environment.

WHAT ARE PROMPTS?

Imagine stepping into a high-stakes negotiation with only half the information—you're likely to miss the mark. Similarly, Chatbots rely on well-crafted prompts to deliver precise and valuable responses.

Prompts serve as the guiding questions, suggestions, or ideas that instruct Chatbots on how and what to respond. But these aren't just any text or phrase; prompts are carefully engineered inputs designed to optimize the Chatbot's output for quality, relevance, and accuracy.

Prompts are suggestions, questions, or ideas for what Chatbots should respond. And for Chatbots to provide a helpful response to their users, they need a thorough prompt with some background information and relevant context. Becoming a solid prompt writer takes time and experience, but there are also some best practices that you can use to see success fairly quickly:

1. **Be precise in your instructions:** When interacting with Chatbots for leadership or coaching tasks, specificity is paramount. Clearly define the tone, scope, and objectives you wish the Chatbot to achieve. For instance, you might say, "Generate a team motivational message that emphasizes the importance of collaboration and aligns with our Q4 targets. Keep the message under 150 words and use a motivational tone."
2. **Integrate contextual information:** The more context you provide, the better Chatbots can tailor their responses. Always include any relevant background information or guidelines. For example, in the case of crafting a message to resolve team conflicts, you may want to append specific issues or arguments that the team is facing.
3. **Segment your interactions:** Complex leadership tasks often have multiple components. Break these down into discrete tasks and use individual prompts for each. If you're generating materials for a leadership workshop, you could use separate prompts for the introduction, body, and conclusion segments.
4. **Continuous refinement:** Chatbots provide a valuable starting point but shouldn't replace your own expertise and voice. Use the generated material as a draft that can be further honed and personalized. This ensures that the content aligns with your unique leadership style and the specific needs of your team or mentees.
5. **Employ follow-up prompts:** To get more nuanced advice, use follow-up prompts based on initial outputs. For example, if your first prompt is, "Outline the key principles for effective leadership," a good follow-up could be, "Explain the application of each principle in remote team settings." This sequencing enriches the dialogue and makes the Chatbot's advice more actionable. Check Appendix No 2 for 1100 follow-up prompts you could use, but remember they also need to be tailored to the specific conversation you are having with the Chatbot.

HOW TO USE THIS BOOK?

In the current professional ecosystem, the topics of coaching, mentoring, and leadership are intricate but filled with unprecedented opportunities. This book offers a comprehensive guide for leveraging artificial intelligence, specifically Chatbots, to gain a competitive edge in these sectors. While the content is structured around key frameworks and principles of leadership and coaching, you are encouraged to engage with this book in a non-linear fashion, focusing on areas most relevant to your immediate and long-term objectives.

1. **Optimize your outcomes with our specialized GPT:** We are thrilled to provide exclusive access to "*My Coaching, Mentoring & Leadership Advisor*" GPT, a cutting-edge tool developed using OpenAI's ChatGPT technology. This custom GPT model is specifically designed to offer targeted assistance in leadership, coaching, and mentoring, enhancing your professional journey with AI-driven insights. To maximize its impact, we recommend using this GPT in conjunction with the prompts provided in this book. This synergistic approach will amplify your learning experience, offering a unique blend of expert guidance and personalized AI assistance. To access this GPT, please refer to the following chapter in this book.

2. **Prompt engineering for optimal outcomes:** We advocate for an informed, strategic approach to using the prompts provided in this book. Each prompt is meticulously engineered to serve a specific purpose and is accompanied by its intended goal, a guiding formula, and two illustrative examples. Text highlighted in **bold** and terms enclosed in square brackets **[ ]** are particularly conducive to customization. We encourage you to not just copy these prompts verbatim but to understand their underlying structure and adapt them to your unique circumstances. The more tailored the prompt, the more relevant and actionable the output will be.

3. **Differentiating complexities for broader utility:** The aim is to offer a broader perspective on how these prompts can be employed and customized. By engaging with a diverse array of prompts, you can develop a nuanced understanding of their underlying mechanisms, thereby gaining the flexibility to tailor them to multiple contexts or objectives.

4. **Integrative strategies for customization:** As you move through this book, you are encouraged to blend different strategies and tools to create customized plans. A well-crafted prompt elicits a higher-quality response; thus, investment in tailoring your inquiries is more than just a recommendation—it's a necessity for meaningful engagement with the book's content.

5. **Ethical considerations and critical thinking:** AI provides valuable insights, but it's crucial to critically evaluate this information. Use Chatbots' advice as a starting point for your strategies, complementing it with further research and ethical considerations. It's essential to remember that while AI can augment decision-making, it can't replace human wisdom.

6. **Communication excellence:** When crafting prompts for Chatbots, aim for clarity and precision. Open-ended questions often lead to more in-depth responses. For a tailored experience, you can also specify the persona or role you want the AI to assume, thereby aligning its feedback with your specific leadership or coaching context.

7. **Target audience, industry, and specificity:** Clearly defining your target audience and industry will enable you to fine-tune the strategies and insights you derive from this book and the accompanying AI resources. Whether you are a leadership consultant, executive coach, or HR professional, audience specificity enhances the utility of the guidance offered.

8. **Getting started with Chatbots:** For those new to the Chatbots platform, we provide a step-by-step guide to get you up and running, empowering you to leverage AI capabilities for your professional development in leadership and coaching.

Here is an overview of the appendices and how they can be integrated into your prompting:

- **Appendix No. 4** - Professions in Mentoring, Coaching, and Leadership: This appendix enumerates key professions that support personal and organizational development through guidance, training, and inspiration. Select the profession most relevant to your current challenge or opportunity to tailor your prompts, ensuring the most pertinent input from the Chatbot.
- **Appendix No. 5** - Specializations in Mentoring, Coaching, and Leadership: This section presents specialized roles within these fields, emphasizing excellence, innovation, and resilience in professional settings. Choose a specialization closely aligned with your specific challenge or opportunity to create effective prompts and receive the most relevant input from the Chatbot.
- **Appendix No. 6** - Tones for Responses from Chatbots: This appendix explores various writing tones you may want Chatbots to use in their responses to your prompts, ensuring alignment with your communication preferences.
- **Appendix No. 7** - Writing Styles for Responses from Chatbots: This section explores a variety of writing styles designed to enhance the clarity and effectiveness of the responses you seek to obtain from Chatbots, ensuring tailored and impactful communication.
- **Appendix No. 8** - Tagging System for Prompt Navigation: This appendix extends beyond the table of contents by offering three tags for each prompt in the book. These tags are carefully selected to assist readers in easily finding the most relevant prompts for their specific challenges or opportunities, ensuring a targeted and efficient use of the book's resources

By strategically integrating AI tools and best practices, you can enhance not just your personal growth, but also the development of those you coach, mentor, and lead.

MEET "MY COACHING, MENTORING & LEADERSHIP ADVISOR" GPT

My Coaching, Mentoring & Leadership Advisor GPT, developed with OpenAI's ChatGPT technology, enhances your interaction with ChatGPT, offering a more tailored and responsive experience.

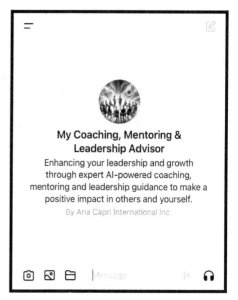

This custom GPT (Generative Pre-trained Transformer) model is expertly crafted to provide targeted help in leadership, coaching, and mentoring.

As a dynamic Artificial Intelligence companion, it aligns with your unique professional style and needs, providing tailored advice and insights to help navigate your leadership path.

Engaging with this GPT is incredibly intuitive, and simpler than you might expect. Once you access to ChatGPT, you'll be greeted by a user-friendly interface where you can input your questions or prompts.

The GPT responds almost instantly, offering valuable insights and guidance.

Whether you aim to enhance your leadership abilities, improve team dynamics, or foster personal and professional growth, *My Coaching, Mentoring & Leadership Advisor GPT* stands as your gateway to innovative professional development.

Accompanying this section is a screenshot showcasing the user interface you'll encounter when accessing 'My Coaching, Mentoring & Leadership Advisor' GPT. This visual reference provides a clear preview of what to expect, guiding you through your first steps in utilizing this innovative tool.

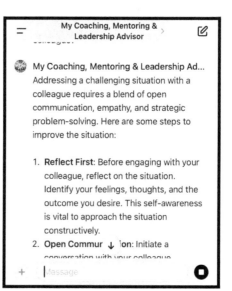

To start your journey towards advanced leadership and coaching skills, and to experience this unique blend of knowledge and technology, please scan this QR code.

Disclaimer: There's a monthly fee for using OpenAI's Plus plan, which you need to access the GPT I created for this book. Wanted to be clear – I don't get any income from OpenAI for suggesting their service. It's all about giving you great tools, and that's why I produced this GPT specifically for the book and for you. As of now, us GPT builders don't get a share of OpenAI's earnings, but if that ever changes – I'll update the disclaimer right away. Mauricio

FREE GOODWILL

Would you consider investing a minute to leave a lasting impression on someone's professional journey? Your experience and insights matter.

Right now, there's a professional, a mentor, or a leader seeking to elevate their capabilities. They're navigating the challenges of leadership, coaching, and perhaps even career transition. Your review could be a pivotal guide for them.

Think of reviews as more than just responses—they're endorsements, collective knowledge, and indicators of reliability. If this book offers you actionable insights or innovative strategies, could you share those experiences through a quick review? By doing so, you contribute to:

- Directing someone to tools and strategies that can heighten their leadership skills.
- Facilitating an individual's capacity to better mentor and coach.
- Enriching someone's perspective, which they might have otherwise overlooked.
- Catalyzing transformation in another's professional path.

By reviewing this book, you contribute to broadening the horizon of effective leadership, mentorship, and coaching for someone else. If you find value in this book, don't hesitate to share it within your network. People remember fondly those who introduced them to beneficial resources.

Enjoyed our book? Scan the QR code to quickly leave a review where you purchased it. Your feedback is invaluable!

Your engagement is much appreciated. Thank you for becoming an advocate for impactful leadership and personal development.

Best regards,

Mauricio

I

Scan the QR code to access our book collection.

TABLE OF CONTENTS

ACCOUNTABILITY...19

ACTION..20

AWARENESS.. 22

BELIEF..27

CHALLENGE...31

CHANGE..36

COMMITMENT..39

CREATIVITY...39

DECISIONS...42

EXCITEMENT.. 43

FEELINGS.. 47

FLOW..50

FULFILLMENT...51

GOALS...52

HABITS..55

LEARNING..56

LISTENING... 63

MINDSET...65

OPTIONS.. 70

PERFORMANCE...73

PREFERENCES... 76

PRIORITIES...77

PROGRESS...78

PURPOSE...80

RELATIONSHIPS... 84

SELF-ASSESSMENT.. 94

SKILLS...97

STRENGTH..100

SUPPORT..107

WEAKNESS..117

ACCOUNTABILITY

<u>PROMPT No 1</u>

Tags

Accountability - Leadership - Performance

<u>Goal</u>

Engage in a transformative process to foster a culture of accountability and ownership within the team, thereby enhancing task completion, work quality, and overall team performance and cohesion.

<u>Prompt</u>

Given the **present challenges** my team faces with **accountability and task ownership,** as a **leadership coach,** could you provide an in-depth exploration of proven strategies and actionable steps to **nurture a culture of responsibility and engagement**? The ultimate aim is to **enhance task adherence, elevate work quality, and foster team harmony,** while maintaining a **supportive and encouraging atmosphere.**

<u>Formula</u>

Given the **[specific challenges]** my team faces with **[issue area]**, as a **[profession]**, could you provide an in-depth exploration of proven strategies and actionable steps to **[desired outcome]**? The ultimate aim is to **[long-term benefits]**, while maintaining a **[desired tone and atmosphere]**.

<u>Examples</u>

Example 1: Given the recurring conflicts my team encounters with communication, as a conflict resolution specialist, could you provide an in-depth exploration of proven strategies and actionable steps to enhance interpersonal understanding and transparency? The ultimate aim is to foster a harmonious work environment, elevate collaborative efforts, and promote a culture of open dialogue, while maintaining a respectful and empathetic atmosphere.

Example 2: Given the stagnation my team experiences with innovation, as an innovation coach, could you provide an in-depth exploration of proven strategies and actionable steps to reignite the creative spark and collaborative spirit? The ultimate aim is to accelerate the generation of novel ideas, foster an enriching brainstorming culture, and enhance project outcomes, while maintaining an inspiring and stimulating atmosphere.

<u>PROMPT No 2</u>

Tags

Team Accountability -   Solution-Oriented - Professional Setting

<u>Goal</u>

To provide a robust methodology for establishing and maintaining accountability, thereby enhancing performance, fostering responsibility, and achieving organizational goals

Prompt

Act as a **Leadership Consultant** with a specialization in **team accountability** in the **aerospace industry**. Could you provide insights on **specific and effective ways that team members can maintain accountability among themselves in a professional setting**? Please include **accountability frameworks, peer-review mechanisms, and communication protocols**. Make sure to cover how **to set clear expectations and how to handle accountability lapses constructively**. Investigate unconventional **accountability practices** and cutting-edge **performance tracking technologies** to **ensure sustained accountability**. Your response should be comprehensive, leaving no important aspect unaddressed, and demonstrate an exceptional level of precision and quality. Let's think about this step by step. Write using a **solution-oriented** tone and a **professional advisory** style.

Act as a **[profession]** with a specialization in **[area of expertise]** in the **[industry]**. Could you provide insights on **[specific challenge/opportunity]**? Please include **[methods/techniques]**. Make sure to cover how **[key areas/topics]**. Investigate unconventional **[area for innovation]** and cutting-edge **[technologies/methods]** to **[desired outcome]**. Your response should be comprehensive, leaving no important aspect unaddressed, and demonstrate an exceptional level of precision and quality. Let's think about this step by step. Write using a **[type]** tone and **[style]** writing style.

Example 1: Act as a Corporate Ethicist with a specialization in ethical accountability in the finance industry. Could you provide insights on specific and effective ways that team members can maintain ethical accountability among themselves in a professional setting? Please include ethical guidelines, whistleblowing mechanisms, and conflict-of-interest policies. Make sure to cover how to establish a culture of ethical responsibility and how to address ethical lapses constructively. Explore the use of blockchain for transparent decision-making and AI-driven ethics training programs. Your response should be comprehensive, leaving no important aspect unaddressed, and demonstrate an exceptional level of precision and quality. Let's think about this step by step. Write using a solution-oriented tone and a professional advisory style.

Example 2: Act as a Team Dynamics Expert with a specialization in remote work accountability in the tech industry. Could you provide insights on specific and effective ways that remote team members can maintain accountability among themselves in a professional setting? Please include virtual check-ins, asynchronous communication tools, and remote team-building exercises. Make sure to cover how to manage time zones and how to maintain work-life balance while ensuring accountability. Delve into gamification techniques and virtual coworking spaces to foster a sense of responsibility. Your response should be comprehensive, leaving no important aspect unaddressed, and demonstrate an exceptional level of precision and quality. Let's think about this step by step. Write using a solution-oriented tone and a professional advisory style.

ACTION

PROMPT No 3

Growth Cultivation - Fulfillment Fostering - Team Development

To gain a detailed understanding of the specific steps that can be implemented to effectively cultivate a growth mindset within a team, fostering a sense of fulfillment and enabling them to achieve their dreams.

As a **Leadership Development Consultant**, adopting an **encouraging and supportive tone**, could you provide a detailed explanation of the precise and comprehensive steps that I can implement to effectively cultivate a **growth mindset** within **my team**? This is particularly relevant given the goal of **fostering a sense of fulfillment and enabling them to achieve their dreams**.

As a **[profession]**, adopting a **[tone of voice]**, could you provide a detailed explanation of the precise and comprehensive steps that **[I/Name/Role]** can implement to effectively cultivate a **[desired outcome]** within **[my/their]** **[team/group/department]**? This is particularly relevant given the goal of **[desired outcome]**.

Example 1: Adopting an encouraging and supportive tone, as a Leadership Development Consultant, could you provide a detailed explanation of the precise and comprehensive steps that a department head can implement to effectively cultivate a growth mindset within their customer service team? This is particularly relevant given the goal of fostering a sense of fulfillment and enabling them to achieve their customers' success KPIs.

Example 2: As a Team Coach, adopting an enthusiastic and optimistic tone, could you provide a detailed explanation of the precise and comprehensive steps that I can implement to effectively cultivate a growth mindset within my project team? This is particularly relevant given the goal of fostering a sense of fulfillment and enabling them to achieve their project dreams.

PROMPT No 4

Management - Diversity - Strategies

To acquire strategies for effectively managing various types of professionals within a team.

Given the challenge of **managing diverse team members**, could you, as an **organizational development consultant** and in a **solution-oriented tone**, explain strategies I could consider to manage them?

Given the challenge of **[contextual challenge/opportunity]**, could you, as a **[profession]** and in a **[tone of voice]**, explain strategies **[I/Name/Role]**'s team could consider to manage their **[suppliers/subordinates/peers]**?

Example 1: Given the challenge of managing international suppliers, could you, as a management consultant and in a clear and concise tone, explain strategies a procurement team could consider?

Example 2: Could you, as a human resources consultant and in an empathetic tone, explain strategies my team could consider to manage their subordinates, especially in the context of a remote working environment?

PROMPT No 5

Tags

Sustainability - Expenses - Debt Mitigation

Goal

To gain a detailed plan of specific initial actions a team can undertake to decrease variable expenses or outstanding debts, fostering financial management and business sustainability.

Prompt

Given the challenge of **decreasing variable expenses or outstanding debts**, as a **Management Consultant** and in a **clear and concise tone**, could you provide a detailed plan of specific initial actions **my team** can undertake?

Formula

Given the challenge of **[contextual challenge/opportunity]**, as a **[profession]** and in a **[tone of voice]**, could you provide a detailed plan of specific initial actions **[my/their] [team/group/department]** can undertake?

Examples

Example 1: Given the challenge of decreasing variable expenses or outstanding debts in a startup environment, as a Business Coach and in a solution-oriented and professional tone, could you provide a detailed plan of specific initial actions a startup founder can have their team undertake?

Example 2: As a Financial Advisor, in a clear and concise tone, could you provide a detailed plan of specific initial actions my finance team can undertake to decrease variable expenses or outstanding debts? This advice is particularly relevant given the challenge of financial management in a competitive market.

AWARENESS

PROMPT No 6

Tags

Self-Awareness - Work Ethic - High-Performance Culture

Goal

To gain detailed recommendations of effective strategies to enhance self-awareness and its influence on work ethic in a team, fostering a high-performance culture and personal growth.

Given the goal of **enhancing self-awareness and its influence on work ethic**, as a **Leadership Development Facilitator** and in an **encouraging and professional tone**, could you provide detailed recommendations of effective strategies I can impart to **my team**?

Given the goal of **[contextual challenge/opportunity]**, as a **[profession]** and in a **[tone of voice]**, could you provide detailed recommendations of effective strategies **[I/Name/Role]** can impart to **[my/their]** **[team/group/department]**?

Example 1: Given the goal of enhancing self-awareness and its influence on work ethic in a dynamic startup environment, as an Executive Coach and in an empowering and supportive tone, could you provide detailed recommendations of effective strategies a startup founder can impart to their team?

Example 2: As a Human Resources (HR) Consultant, in a respectful and clear tone, could you provide detailed recommendations of effective strategies I can impart to my marketing team to enhance their self-awareness and its influence on their work ethic? This advice is particularly relevant given the goal of fostering a high-performance culture.

PROMPT No 7

Autonomous Assessment - Training Effectiveness - Work Enhancement

To equip team leaders, and professionals with a comprehensive approach for training team members effectively, with a focus on empowering them to autonomously assess their work and identify areas for improvement.

Act as a **Training and Development Specialist** with a specialization in **self-assessment and skill enhancement** in the **manufacturing industry**. Could you provide specific strategies and methods that can be employed **to train my team members effectively**? This is particularly relevant given the goal of **empowering them to autonomously assess their own work and recognize areas that need enhancement**. Please include **competency frameworks, self-assessment tools, and feedback loops**. Make sure to cover how **to set performance benchmarks and how to foster a culture of continuous improvement**. Investigate unconventional **training methodologies** and cutting-edge **e-learning platforms** to **facilitate self-assessment**. Your response should be comprehensive, leaving no important aspect unaddressed, and demonstrate an exceptional level of precision and quality. Let's think about this step by step. Write using a **supportive and instructive** tone and a **skill-building guide** style.

Act as a [profession] with a specialization in [area of expertise] in the [industry]. Could you provide specific strategies and methods that can be employed to [specific challenge/opportunity]? This is particularly relevant given the goal of [specific goal]. Please include [methods/techniques]. Make sure to cover how [key areas/topics]. Investigate unconventional [area for innovation] and cutting-edge [technologies/methods] to [desired outcome]. Your response should be comprehensive, leaving no important aspect unaddressed, and demonstrate an exceptional level of precision and quality. Let's think about this step by step. Write using a [type] tone and [style] writing style.

Example 1: Act as a Training and Development Specialist with a specialization in remote work training in the tech industry. Adopting a supportive and instructive tone, could you provide specific strategies and methods that can be employed to train my remote team members effectively? This is particularly relevant given the goal of empowering them to autonomously assess their own work and recognize areas that need enhancement. Please include virtual training modules, time management tools, and remote team-building exercises. Make sure to cover how to set remote work KPIs and how to use virtual feedback mechanisms. Explore the use of VR training simulations and AI-driven self-assessment tools. Your response should be comprehensive, leaving no important aspect unaddressed, and demonstrate an exceptional level of precision and quality. Let's think about this step by step. Write using a supportive and instructive tone and a skill-building guide style.

Example 2: Act as a Training and Development Specialist with a specialization in leadership development in the healthcare industry. Adopting a supportive and instructive tone, could you provide specific strategies and methods that can be employed to train my healthcare leadership team effectively? This is particularly relevant given the goal of empowering them to autonomously assess their own work and recognize areas that need enhancement. Please include leadership competency models, 360-degree feedback tools, and mentorship programs. Make sure to cover how to set leadership performance metrics and how to foster a culture of self-improvement. Delve into the use of gamified training platforms and real-time performance analytics. Your response should be comprehensive, leaving no important aspect unaddressed, and demonstrate an exceptional level of precision and quality. Let's think about this step by step. Write using a supportive and instructive tone and a skill-building guide style.

PROMPT No 8

Mission Influence - Organizational Culture - Team Mindset

To understand the influence of a company's mission or vision on a team's thinking patterns and overall mindset.

Given the significant role a **company's mission or vision plays in shaping its culture**, could you, as an **organizational development consultant** and in an **insightful tone**, discuss how these elements influence **my team's thinking patterns**?

Given the significant role of **[contextual challenge/opportunity]**, could you, as a **[profession]** and in a **[tone of voice]**, discuss how these elements influence **[I/Name/Role]**'s team's **[desired outcome]**?

Example 1: Given the significant role a company's mission plays in shaping its culture, could you, as a Leadership Trainer and in an insightful tone, discuss how this element influences a project team's thinking patterns?

Example 2: Could you, as a corporate trainer and in a clear and concise tone, discuss how the vision of the company influences my team's thinking patterns, especially considering the significant role such elements play in shaping organizational culture?

PROMPT No 9

Cohesive Culture - Organizational Success - Mission Cultivation

To gain detailed and comprehensive recommendations for the most effective and efficient strategies and techniques companies can implement to cultivate a strong and cohesive culture or mission, fostering organizational success and cohesion.

Considering the importance of **cultivating a strong and cohesive culture or mission within an organization**, as an **Organizational Development (OD) Consultant** and in an **inspirational and professional tone**, could you provide detailed and comprehensive recommendations for the most effective and efficient strategies and techniques **companies** can implement?

Considering the importance of **[contextual challenge/opportunity]**, as a **[profession]** and in a **[tone of voice]**, could you provide detailed and comprehensive recommendations for the most effective and efficient strategies and techniques **[companies/organizations]** can implement?

Example 1: Considering the importance of cultivating a strong and cohesive culture or mission within a startup, as a Business Coach and in an encouraging and optimistic tone, could you provide detailed and comprehensive recommendations for the most effective and efficient strategies and techniques startups can implement?

Example 2: As a Leadership Development Consultant, in a motivational and professional tone, could you provide detailed and comprehensive recommendations for the most effective and efficient strategies and techniques a non-profit organization can implement to cultivate a strong and cohesive culture or mission? This advice is particularly relevant considering the importance of a strong mission in a non-profit environment.

PROMPT No 10

Tags

Resilience - Virtue - Communication

Goal

To gain insights on how to effectively communicate to a team the importance of developing self-control and resilience to overcome negative emotions, while emphasizing the crucial role of virtue in promoting happiness.

Prompt

As a **Leadership Development Consultant**, adopting a **supportive and encouraging tone**, could you provide specific methods or approaches that **I** can employ to ensure that **I** effectively convey to **my team** the importance of **developing self-control and fortitude to overcome harmful emotions**? Additionally, how can **I** effectively emphasize the **pivotal role of virtue in fostering happiness**?

Formula

As a **[profession]**, adopting a **[tone of voice]**, could you provide specific methods or approaches that **[I/Name/Role]** can employ to ensure that **[I/Name/Role]** effectively convey to **[my/their]** **[team/group/department]** the importance of **[contextual challenge/opportunity]**? Additionally, how can **[I/Name/Role]** effectively emphasize the **[contextual challenge/opportunity]**?

Examples

Example 1: As a Team Coach, adopting a compassionate and understanding tone, could you provide specific methods or approaches that a department head can employ to ensure that they effectively convey to their faculty the importance of developing self-control and fortitude to overcome harmful emotions? Additionally, how can they effectively emphasize the pivotal role of virtue in fostering happiness?

Example 2: As a Human Resources (HR) Consultant, adopting a clear and concise tone, could you provide specific methods or approaches that I can employ to ensure that I effectively convey to my project team the importance of developing self-control and fortitude to overcome harmful emotions? Additionally, how can I effectively emphasize the pivotal role of virtue in fostering happiness?

PROMPT No 11

Tags

Reflection - Growth - Learning

Goal

To gain insights on how to guide a team to see the potential for learning and growth even when they do not achieve their desired outcome or solution. This involves fostering a mindset that values the process and the insights gained from it, not just the end result.

As a **Leadership Development Consultant**, adopting a **supportive and encouraging tone**, could you provide effective strategies to encourage **my team** to engage in reflection and consider the potential for gaining new insights and understanding when they do not achieve their **desired outcome or solution**?

As a **[profession]**, adopting a **[tone of voice]**, could you provide effective strategies to encourage **[my/their]** **[team/group/department]** to engage in reflection and consider the potential for gaining new insights and understanding when they do not achieve their **[contextual challenge/opportunity]**?

Example 1: As a Team Coach, adopting a supportive and encouraging tone, could you provide effective strategies to encourage my project team to engage in reflection and consider the potential for gaining new insights and understanding when they do not achieve their project goals?

Example 2: As a Management Consultant, adopting a supportive and encouraging tone, could you provide effective strategies to encourage the IT department to engage in reflection and consider the potential for gaining new insights and understanding when they do not achieve their software development goals?

BELIEF

PROMPT No 12

Assessment - Workload - Balance

To gain a comprehensive understanding of the specific steps that can be taken to thoroughly assess whether a team is efficiently handling their workload and responsibilities, and if they are maintaining a healthy work-life balance.

As a **Human Resources Consultant**, adopting a **supportive and professional tone**, could you guide **me** on the specific steps **I** can take to thoroughly assess whether **my team** is efficiently handling their **workload and responsibilities**, and if they are maintaining a **healthy work-life balance**? Please provide a comprehensive explanation with detailed actions to follow.

As a **[profession]**, adopting a **[tone of voice]**, could you guide **[me/Name/Role]** on the specific steps **[I/Name/Role]** can take to thoroughly assess whether **[my/their]** **[team/group/department]** is efficiently handling their **[contextual challenge/opportunity]**, and if they are maintaining **[desired outcome]**? Please provide a comprehensive explanation with detailed actions to follow.

Examples

Example 1: As a Team Coach, adopting an empathetic and understanding tone, could you guide me on the specific steps I can take to thoroughly assess whether my sales team is efficiently handling their client portfolio and responsibilities, and if they are maintaining a healthy work-life balance? Please provide a comprehensive explanation with detailed actions to follow.

Example 2: As a Leadership Development Consultant, adopting a clear and concise tone, could you guide a department head on the specific steps they can take to thoroughly assess whether their faculty is efficiently handling their academic workload and responsibilities, and if they are maintaining a healthy work-life balance? Please provide a comprehensive explanation with detailed actions to follow.

PROMPT No 13

Tags

Alignment - Work-Ethic - Productivity

Goal

To gain insights on effective strategies and methods that can be utilized to align the beliefs and work ethic of a team with their actions, and vice versa, ensuring a harmonious and productive work environment.

Prompt

As a **Leadership Development Consultant**, adopting a **supportive and insightful tone**, could you provide an in-depth explanation of the strategies and methods that can be utilized to **effectively align the beliefs and work ethic** of **my team** with their actions? Additionally, could you elaborate on the approaches that can be employed to ensure that their actions remain in sync with their beliefs and work ethic? This is particularly relevant given the goal of creating a harmonious and productive work environment.

Formula

As a **[profession]**, adopting a **[tone of voice]**, could you provide an in-depth explanation of the strategies and methods that can be utilized to **[contextual challenge/opportunity]** of **[my/their] [team/group/department]** with their actions? Additionally, could you elaborate on the approaches that can be employed to **[contextual challenge/opportunity]**? This is particularly relevant given the goal of **[desired outcome]**.

Examples

Example 1: As a Team Coach, adopting a collaborative and professional tone, could you provide an in-depth explanation of the strategies and methods that can be utilized to effectively align the beliefs and work ethic of my sales team with their actions? Additionally, could you elaborate on the approaches that can be employed to ensure that their actions remain in sync with their beliefs and work ethic? This is particularly relevant given the goal of enhancing sales performance and team cohesion.

Example 2: As an HR Consultant, adopting a clear and concise tone, could you provide an in-depth explanation of the strategies and methods that can be utilized to effectively align the beliefs and work ethic of the marketing department with their actions? Additionally, could you elaborate on the approaches that can be employed to ensure that their actions remain in sync with their beliefs and work ethic? This is particularly relevant given the goal of improving departmental performance and employee satisfaction.

PROMPT No 14

Tags
Improvement - Change - Mindset

Goal
To obtain practical steps for changing a team's fixed mindset and fostering a belief in the potential for improvement and change.

Prompt
Considering the challenge of **overcoming a fixed mindset in a team**, could you, as a **performance coach** and in an **empowering tone**, provide practical steps I could take to change my **team's** belief that their **work** can't **improve or change**?

Formula
Considering the challenge of **[contextual challenge/opportunity]**, could you, as a **[profession]** and in a **[tone of voice]**, provide practical steps **[I/Name/Role]** could take to change **[team/group/department]**'s belief that their **[work/performance/results]** can't **[improve/change/evolve]**?

Examples
Example 1: Considering the challenge of overcoming a stagnant mindset in a sales team, could you, as a business coach and in a motivational tone, provide practical steps a sales manager could take to change their team's belief that their sales performance can't improve?
Example 2: Could you, as a leadership development consultant and in an optimistic tone, provide practical steps I could take to change my project team's belief that their project outcomes can't change, especially considering the challenge of overcoming a fixed mindset?

PROMPT No 15

Tags
Communication - Losses - Commitment

Goal

To gain insights on how to improve communication within the team and conduct a comprehensive evaluation of potential losses in the team's current situation.

As a **Communication Consultant**, adopting a **solution-oriented and empathetic tone**, could you provide specific tactics or methods that **I** can utilize to improve communication and ensure a comprehensive assessment of potential losses in my team's present situation regarding **their lack of commitment to work?**

As a **[profession]**, adopting a **[tone of voice]**, could you provide specific tactics or methods that **[I/Name/Role]** can utilize to improve communication and ensure a comprehensive assessment of potential losses in **[my/their]** **[team/group/department]**'s present situation regarding **[contextual challenge/opportunity]?**

Example 1: As a Business Consultant, adopting a strategic and supportive tone, could you provide specific tactics or methods that a construction manager can utilize to improve communication and ensure a comprehensive assessment of potential missed opportunities in their project team's present situation regarding their lack of proper planning?

Example 2: As a Team Coach, adopting a proactive and understanding tone, could you provide specific tactics or methods that I can utilize to improve communication and ensure a comprehensive assessment of potential losses in my IT team's present situation regarding their lack of oversight on their projects?

PROMPT No 16

Beliefs - Progress - Work

To gain insight into the beliefs about work that might be preventing a team from moving forward, fostering an understanding of limiting beliefs and how they impact team progress.

As a **Career Coach**, adopting a **patient and empathetic tone**, could you describe the **beliefs about work** that might be preventing **my team** from moving forward? This is particularly relevant given the challenge of overcoming limiting beliefs to enhance team progress.

As a **[profession]**, adopting a **[tone of voice]**, could you describe the **[contextual challenge/opportunity]** that might be preventing **[my/their]** **[team/group/department]** from moving forward? This is particularly relevant given the **[contextual challenge/opportunity]**.

Example 1: Adopting a respectful and supportive tone, as a Leadership Development Facilitator, could you describe the beliefs about academic work that might be preventing a faculty from moving forward? This is particularly relevant given the challenge of overcoming limiting beliefs to enhance academic progress.

Example 2: As a Performance Coach, adopting a clear and concise tone, could you describe the beliefs about project work that might be preventing my project team from moving forward? This is particularly relevant given the challenge of overcoming limiting beliefs to enhance project progress.

PROMPT No 17

Tags

Evolution - Beliefs - Identification

Goal

To gain insights on how to identify the beliefs that the team used to hold but no longer consider to be true, in order to understand their evolving perspectives and adapt leadership strategies accordingly.

Prompt

As a **Leadership Development Consultant**, adopting a **respectful and empathetic tone**, could you provide me with strategies and methods to effectively identify the **beliefs that my team used to hold but no longer consider to be true at present**?

Formula

As a **[profession]**, adopting a **[tone of voice]**, could you provide **[me/Name/Role]** with strategies and methods to effectively identify the **[contextual challenge/opportunity]**?

Examples

Example 1: As a Human Resources (HR) Consultant, adopting a respectful and empathetic tone, could you provide a department head with strategies and methods to effectively identify the beliefs that their faculty used to hold but no longer consider to be true at present? **Example 2:** As a Leadership Coach, adopting a respectful and empathetic tone, could you provide me with strategies and methods to effectively identify the beliefs that my project team used to hold but no longer consider to be true at present?

CHALLENGE

PROMPT No 18

Tags

Solutions - Proactivity - Challenges

Goal

To gain a comprehensive list of specific actions that can be implemented by a team to effectively address and overcome new challenges they are currently facing.

As a **Team Development Consultant**, adopting a **solution-oriented and proactive tone**, could you provide a detailed and comprehensive list of specific actions that **my team** can implement in order to effectively address and overcome the **new challenges we are currently encountering**?

As a **[profession]**, adopting a **[tone of voice]**, could you provide a detailed and comprehensive list of specific actions that **[our/my/their]** **[team/group/department]** can implement in order to effectively address and overcome the **[contextual challenge/opportunity]** we are currently encountering?

Example 1: As a Business Strategy Consultant, adopting a strategic and forward-thinking tone, could you provide a detailed and comprehensive list of specific actions that our sales team can implement in order to effectively address and overcome the new market challenges with lower sales volume we are currently encountering?

Example 2: As a Change Management Consultant, adopting a supportive and empathetic tone, could you provide a detailed and comprehensive list of specific actions that our HR department can implement in order to effectively address and overcome the new organizational changes with lack of engagement from our workforce we are currently encountering?

PROMPT No 19

Exploration - Diversity - Analysis

To gain a comprehensive understanding of specific strategies, techniques, or methods that can be utilized to effectively encourage and facilitate a team's exploration of various perspectives and approaches when analyzing a problem.

As a **Problem-Solving Expert**, adopting a **solution-oriented and analytical tone**, could you please provide a detailed explanation of the specific strategies, techniques, or methods that **I** can employ to effectively **encourage and facilitate my team's exploration of diverse perspectives and approaches** when **analyzing a problem**?

As a **[profession]**, adopting a **[tone of voice]**, could you please provide a detailed explanation of the specific strategies, techniques, or methods that **[I/Name/Role]** can employ to effectively **[desired outcome]** when **[contextual challenge/opportunity]**?

Example 1: As a Team Development Coach, adopting a supportive and encouraging tone, could you please provide a detailed explanation of the specific strategies, techniques, or methods that a project manager can employ to effectively encourage and facilitate their team's exploration of diverse perspectives and approaches when analyzing project-related problems?

Example 2: As a Leadership Consultant, adopting a clear and concise tone, could you please provide a detailed explanation of the specific strategies, techniques, or methods that I can employ to effectively encourage and facilitate my marketing team's exploration of diverse perspectives and approaches when analyzing market-related problems?

PROMPT No 20

Tags

Development - Growth - Challenges

Goal

To gain specific actions and strategies for designing a thorough and effective development plan for a team, enabling them to perceive challenges as opportunities for personal and professional growth and enhancement.

Prompt

As a **Leadership Development Consultant**, adopting a **solution-oriented and supportive tone**, could you guide me through the specific actions and strategies I should implement in order to design a **thorough and effective development plan** for my team? This plan should enable them to perceive challenges as **chances for personal and professional growth and enhancement.**

Formula

As a **[profession]**, adopting a **[tone of voice]**, could you guide me through the specific actions and strategies **[I/Name/Role]** should implement in order to design a **[contextual challenge/opportunity]** for **[my/their]** **[team/group/department]**? This plan should enable them to perceive challenges as **[desired outcome]**.

Examples

Example 1: As a Team Coach, adopting a motivational and supportive tone, could you guide me through the specific actions and strategies I should implement in order to design a thorough and effective development plan for my operations management team? This plan should enable them to perceive challenges as opportunities for personal growth and operations performance enhancement.

Example 2: As a Business Mentor, adopting a solution-oriented and encouraging tone, could you guide a department head through the specific actions and strategies they should implement in order to design a thorough and effective development plan for their faculty? This plan should enable them to perceive challenges as opportunities for professional growth and academic performance enhancement.

PROMPT No 21

Adaptation - Transition - Techniques

To gain specific techniques or habits that individuals can develop and adopt when preparing to confront a fresh challenge or assume a new role, with the aim of facilitating a smooth transition and improving adaptability.

As a **Career Coach**, adopting a **supportive and encouraging tone**, could you recommend specific techniques or habits that individuals can develop and adopt when **getting ready to confront a fresh challenge or assume a new role**? These suggestions should aim to facilitate a smooth transition and improve one's ability to adapt effectively.

As a **[profession]**, adopting a **[tone of voice]**, could you recommend specific techniques or habits that individuals can develop and adopt when **[contextual challenge/opportunity]**? These suggestions should aim to **[desired outcome]**.

Example 1: As a Leadership Development Consultant, adopting a motivational and professional tone, could you recommend specific techniques or habits that a newly promoted manager can develop and adopt when getting ready to confront the fresh challenge of leading a larger team? These suggestions should aim to facilitate a smooth transition and improve the manager's ability to adapt effectively.

Example 2: As a Transition Coach, adopting a patient and understanding tone, could you recommend specific techniques or habits that an individual can develop and adopt when preparing to assume a new role in a different industry? These suggestions should aim to facilitate a smooth transition and improve the individual's ability to adapt effectively.

PROMPT No 22

Team-Leadership - Strategies - Professional-Development

To equip Leadership Coaches, team leaders, and organizational decision-makers with a robust strategy for encouraging teams to view situations or challenges from alternative viewpoints, thereby fostering a culture of diverse thinking and enhanced problem-solving.

Act as a **Leadership Coach** with a specialization in **cognitive diversity and problem-solving** in the **renewable energy industry**. Could you suggest specific tactics or methods that I can implement to **encourage my team to view situations or challenges from alternative viewpoints**? This is particularly relevant given the goal of **fostering a culture of diverse thinking**. Please include **lateral thinking exercises, perspective-shifting workshops, and cognitive diversity assessments**. Make sure to cover how **to facilitate inclusive discussions** and how **to measure the impact of diverse thinking on team performance**. Investigate **unconventional problem-solving techniques and cutting-edge diversity analytics tools** to **enrich team dynamics**. Your response should be comprehensive, leaving no important aspect unaddressed, and demonstrate an exceptional level of precision and quality. Let's think about this step by step. Write using an **open-minded and supportive** tone and a **diversity-enhancing** guide style.

Act as a **[profession]** with a specialization in **[area of expertise]** in the **[industry]**. Could you suggest specific tactics or methods that I can implement to **[specific challenge/opportunity]**? This is particularly relevant given the goal of **[specific goal]**. Please include **[methods/techniques]**. Make sure to cover how **[key areas/topics]**. Investigate **[technologies/methods]** to **[desired outcome]**. Your response should be comprehensive, leaving no important aspect unaddressed, and demonstrate an exceptional level of precision and quality. Let's think about this step by step. Write using a **[type]** tone and **[style]** writing style.

Example 1: Act as a Leadership Coach with a specialization in emotional intelligence in the healthcare industry. Could you suggest specific tactics or methods that I can implement to encourage my nursing team to view patient care challenges from alternative viewpoints? This is particularly relevant given the goal of fostering a culture of diverse thinking. Please include empathy circles, case study discussions, and emotional intelligence assessments. Make sure to cover how to encourage active listening and how to evaluate the emotional impact of diverse viewpoints on patient outcomes. Explore the use of VR empathy training and AI-driven emotional analytics. Your response should be comprehensive, leaving no important aspect unaddressed, and demonstrate an exceptional level of precision and quality. Let's think about this step by step. Write using an open-minded and supportive tone and a diversity-enhancing guide style.

Example 2: Act as a Leadership Coach with a specialization in innovation management in the automotive industry. Could you suggest specific tactics or methods that I can implement to encourage my engineering team to view design challenges from alternative viewpoints? This is particularly relevant given the goal of fostering a culture of diverse thinking. Please include design thinking workshops, cross-disciplinary brainstorming sessions, and innovation metrics. Make sure to cover how to integrate external perspectives and how to track the ROI of diverse thinking in product development. Delve into the use of crowdsourcing for idea generation and blockchain for transparent innovation tracking. Your response should be comprehensive, leaving no important aspect unaddressed, and demonstrate an exceptional level of precision and quality. Let's think about this step by step. Write using an open-minded and supportive tone and a diversity-enhancing guide style.

Tags

Productive-Discussion - Impediment - Insight

Goal

To gain specific strategies and approaches to enhance the ability to have productive and insightful discussions with a team about the factors that have impeded their progress or work towards achieving their goals.

Prompt

As a **Leadership Development Consultant**, adopting a **supportive and understanding tone**, could you provide specific strategies and approaches that **I** can employ to enhance **my** ability to have productive and insightful discussions with **my team** about the factors that have impeded their **progress or work towards achieving their goals?**

Formula

As a **[profession]**, adopting a **[tone of voice]**, could you provide specific strategies and approaches that **[I/Name/Role]** can employ to enhance **[my/their]** ability to have productive and insightful discussions with **[my/their]** **[team/group/department]** about the factors that have impeded their **[contextual challenge/opportunity]**?

Examples

Example 1: As a Team Coach, adopting a patient and empathetic tone, could you provide specific strategies and approaches that a department head can employ to enhance their ability to have productive and insightful discussions with their faculty about the factors that have impeded their academic progress or work towards achieving their teaching goals? **Example 2:** As a Business Coach, adopting a respectful and professional tone, could you provide specific strategies and approaches that I can employ to enhance my ability to have productive and insightful discussions with my project team about the factors that have impeded their project progress or work towards achieving their project goals?

CHANGE

PROMPT No 24

Tags

Diplomacy - Communication - Team-Feedback

Goal

To gain strategies for effectively and tactfully addressing aspects of a situation or project that did not go well with a team, without making them feel defensive or threatened.

Prompt

As a **Leadership Development Consultant**, adopting a **diplomatic and understanding tone**, could you suggest strategies that **I** can employ to effectively and tactfully address the aspects of a **situation or project** that did not go well with **my team**, without making them feel defensive or threatened by **my** approach? This is particularly relevant given the goal of **maintaining a positive and open communication environment**.

As a **[profession]**, adopting a **[tone of voice]**, could you suggest strategies that **[I/Name/Role]** can employ to effectively and tactfully address the aspects of a **[contextual challenge/opportunity]** that did not go well with **[my/their] [team/group/department]**, without making them feel defensive or threatened by **[my/their]** approach? This is particularly relevant given the goal of **[desired outcome]**.

Example 1: As a Team Coach, adopting a respectful and empathetic tone, could you suggest strategies that a logistic department head can employ to effectively and tactfully address the aspects of a procurement project that did not go well with their logistic team, without making them feel defensive or threatened by their approach? This is particularly relevant given the goal of maintaining a positive and open communication environment within the team.

Example 2: As a Human Resources (HR) Consultant, adopting a professional and understanding tone, could you suggest strategies that I can employ to effectively and tactfully address the aspects of a recent restructuring that did not go well with my project team, without making them feel defensive or threatened by my approach? This is particularly relevant given the goal of maintaining a positive and open communication environment within the project team.

PROMPT No 25

Skills-Assessment - Implementation - Team-Development

To gain specific strategies for thoroughly assessing the existing abilities and skills of a team, and to understand how to effectively utilize these capacities to successfully implement any required modifications or improvements.

As a **Team Development Specialist**, adopting a **solution-oriented tone**, could you suggest specific strategies to thoroughly assess the existing abilities and skills of **my team**? Additionally, how can we effectively utilize these capacities to successfully implement any required **modifications or improvements**?

As a **[profession]**, adopting a **[tone of voice]**, could you suggest specific strategies to thoroughly assess the existing abilities and skills of **[my/their] [team/group/department]**? Additionally, how can we effectively utilize these capacities to successfully implement any required **[contextual challenge/opportunity]**?

Examples

Example 1: As a Leadership Development Consultant, adopting a clear and concise tone, could you suggest specific strategies to thoroughly assess the existing abilities and skills of my senior management team? Additionally, how can they effectively utilize these capacities to successfully implement any required strategic modifications or improvements?

Example 2: As a Business Coach, adopting a supportive and encouraging tone, could you suggest specific strategies to thoroughly assess the existing abilities and skills of my risk management team? Additionally, how can we effectively utilize these capacities to successfully implement any required enterprise risk management program improvement?

PROMPT No 26

Tags

Development - Skills - Adaptability

Goal

To gain insights on identifying areas for ongoing development within a team, enhancing their skills and adaptability.

Prompt

As a **talent development specialist**, in an **encouraging and supportive tone**, could you help **me** in identifying the areas of ongoing development for **my team**, particularly in the context of a **rapidly evolving industry**?

Formula

As a **[profession]**, in a **[tone of voice]**, could you help **[I/Name/Role]** in identifying the areas of ongoing development for **[my/their]** **[team/group/department]**, particularly in the context of **[contextual challenge/opportunity]**?

Examples

Example 1: In the context of a rapidly changing tech industry, as a learning and development specialist and in an optimistic and enthusiastic tone, could you help a tech team leader in identifying the areas of ongoing development for their team?

Example 2: As a career coach, in a patient and empathetic tone, could you help me in identifying the areas of ongoing development for my sales team, particularly in the context of a highly competitive market?

COMMITMENT

PROMPT No 27

Tags

Engagement - Productivity - Remote-Work

Goal

To gain insights on measures to implement in order to support a team's commitment to their work, enhancing their engagement and productivity.

Prompt

As a **leadership development manager**, in a **clear and concise tone**, could you outline what measures I could implement to support **my team's** commitment to their work, particularly in the context of a **remote working environment**?

Formula

As a **[profession]**, in a **[tone of voice]**, could you outline what measures **[I/Name/Role]** could implement to support **[my/their]** **[team/group/department]**'s commitment to their **[work/tasks/projects]**, particularly in the context of **[contextual challenge/opportunity]**?

Examples

Example 1: In the context of a remote working environment, as a human resources consultant and in a supportive and understanding tone, could you outline what measures a team leader could implement to support their team's commitment to their tasks?

Example 2: As a performance management specialist, in a professional and solution-oriented tone, could you outline what measures I could implement to support my project team's commitment to their projects, particularly in the context of tight deadlines?

CREATIVITY

PROMPT No 28

Tags

Collaboration - Innovation - Originality

Goal

To gain specific techniques, approaches, and actions to foster effective collaboration with a team, enabling the generation of innovative and original ideas for projects or tasks, fostering effective collaboration and innovation within the team.

Prompt

As a **Change Management Consultant**, adopting a **collaborative and solution-oriented tone**, could you provide specific techniques, approaches, and actions that **I** can utilize to foster effective collaboration with **my team**, enabling us to generate **innovative and original ideas for our projects**

or tasks? This is particularly relevant given the goal of fostering effective collaboration and innovation within the team.

As a **[profession]**, adopting a **[tone of voice]**, could you provide specific techniques, approaches, and actions that **[I/Name/Role]** can utilize to foster effective collaboration with **[my/their] [team/group/department]**, enabling us to generate **[contextual challenge/opportunity]**? This is particularly relevant given the goal of **[desired outcome]**.

Example 1: Adopting a clear and concise tone, as a Management Consultant, could you provide specific techniques, approaches, and actions that a department head can utilize to foster effective collaboration with their IT team, enabling them to generate innovative and original ideas for their research projects? This is particularly relevant given the goal of fostering effective collaboration and innovation within the IT personnel.

Example 2: As a Leadership Trainer, adopting an enthusiastic and professional tone, could you provide specific techniques, approaches, and actions that I can utilize to foster effective collaboration with my project team, enabling us to generate innovative and original ideas for our upcoming project? This is particularly relevant given the goal of fostering effective collaboration and innovation within the project team.

PROMPT No 29

Productivity - Behavior - Performance

To gain specific methods to accurately identify and establish correlations between the productivity and behavior patterns exhibited by team members, with respect to their job performance, understanding the relationship between productivity, behavior patterns, and job performance.

As a **Performance Management Specialist**, adopting a **clear and concise tone**, could you provide specific methods that **I** can employ to accurately identify and establish correlations between the **productivity** and **behavior patterns** exhibited by **my team members**, with respect to their job performance? This is particularly relevant given the goal of **understanding the relationship between productivity, behavior patterns, and job performance**.

As a **[profession]**, adopting a **[tone of voice]**, could you provide specific methods that **[I/Name/Role]** can employ to accurately identify and establish correlations between the **[contextual challenge/opportunity]** and **[contextual challenge/opportunity]** exhibited by **[my/their] [team/group/department]**, with respect to their job performance? This is particularly relevant given the goal of **[desired outcome]**.

Example 1: Adopting a professional and respectful tone, as a Talent Management Specialist, could you provide specific methods that a department head can employ to accurately identify and establish correlations between the productivity and behavior patterns exhibited by their faculty, with respect to their job performance? This is particularly relevant given the goal of understanding the relationship between productivity, behavior patterns, and job performance.

Example 2: As a Human Resources Consultant, adopting a supportive and diplomatic tone, could you provide specific methods that I can employ to accurately identify and establish correlations between the productivity and behavior patterns exhibited by my project team, with respect to their job performance? This is particularly relevant given the goal of understanding the relationship between productivity, behavior patterns, and job performance.

PROMPT No 30

Tags

Creativity - Connection - Inspiration

Goal

To design specific activities that will allow a team to fully harness their creative abilities and foster a deep connection with their innate source of inspiration, fostering creativity and connection within the team.

Prompt

As a **Creative Director**, adopting an **inspiring and innovative tone**, could you suggest how **I** can design specific activities that will allow **my team** to **fully harness their creative abilities** and foster a **deep connection with their innate source of inspiration?** This is particularly relevant given the goal of **fostering creativity and connection within the team.**

Formula

As a **[profession]**, adopting a **[tone of voice]**, could you suggest how **[I/Name/Role]** can design specific activities that will allow **[my/their]** **[team/group/department]** to **[contextual challenge/opportunity]** and **[contextual challenge/opportunity]**? This is particularly relevant given the goal of **[desired outcome]**.

Examples

Example 1: As a Team Building Coach, adopting an engaging and motivational tone, could you suggest how a department head can design specific activities that will allow their faculty to fully harness their creative abilities and foster a deep connection with their innate source of inspiration? This is particularly relevant given the goal of fostering creativity and connection within the faculty.

Example 2: As a Team Development Specialist, adopting a supportive and encouraging tone, could you suggest how I can design specific activities that will allow my marketing team to fully harness their creative abilities and foster a deep connection with their innate source of inspiration? This is particularly relevant given the goal of fostering creativity and connection within the marketing team.

DECISIONS

Data-Driven - Accuracy - Integration

Goal

To systematically and reliably enable data-driven corporate strategies through insightful tactics, ensuring seamless integration into organizational operations.

Prompt

As a **Business Intelligence Consultant** specializing in **data analytics** within the **technology industry**, could you provide an exhaustive and meticulous examination, incorporating innovative insights and inventive strategies, for the specific tactics that ensure accurate and reliable data-driven decisions for shaping a new **corporate strategy**? Additionally, how to disseminate these plans through different team levels and secure buy-in from stakeholders? Advocate for disruptive strategies and unorthodox viewpoints.

Formula

As a [**profession**] specializing in [**area of expertise/focus**] within the [**industry**], could you provide an exhaustive and meticulous examination, incorporating innovative insights and inventive strategies, for the specific tactics that ensure accurate and reliable data-driven decisions for shaping a new [**type of strategy**]? Additionally, how to disseminate these plans through different team levels and secure buy-in from stakeholders? Advocate for disruptive strategies and unorthodox viewpoints.

Examples

Example 1: As an Operations Manager specializing in supply chain logistics within the retail industry, could you provide an exhaustive and meticulous examination, incorporating innovative insights and inventive strategies, for actionable guidelines that ensure streamlined operations for the rollout of a new inventory management system? Additionally, how to disseminate these plans through different team levels and secure buy-in from stakeholders? Unearth hidden gems and non-traditional methods.

Example 2: As a Financial Analyst specializing in investment strategies within the banking sector, could you provide an exhaustive and meticulous examination, incorporating innovative insights and inventive strategies, for investment approaches that maximize shareholder value while mitigating risks? Additionally, how to disseminate these plans through different team levels and secure buy-in from stakeholders? Navigate through unexplored realms and revolutionary paradigms.

PROMPT No 32

Leadership - Empowerment - Positivity

Goal

To gain specific strategies that can be implemented to ensure effective leadership and empowerment of a team, allowing them to independently identify and implement the most impactful methods to foster a positive and enthusiastic mindset towards work.

As a **Leadership Development Consultant**, adopting an **empowering and enthusiastic tone**, could you suggest specific strategies that **I** can implement to ensure **effective leadership and empowerment of my team**? How can **I** enable **them** to independently identify and implement the most impactful methods to **foster a positive and enthusiastic mindset towards work**?

As a **[profession]**, adopting a **[tone of voice]**, could you suggest specific strategies that **[I/Name/Role]** can implement to ensure **[desired outcome]**? How can **[I/Name/Role]** enable **[my/their]** **[team/group/department]** to independently identify and implement the most impactful methods to **[contextual challenge/opportunity]**?

Example 1: As a Team Coach, adopting a motivating and positive tone, could you suggest specific strategies that a finance manager can implement to ensure effective leadership and empowerment of their finance team? How can they enable the team to independently identify and implement the most impactful methods to foster a positive and enthusiastic mindset towards finance reporting tasks?

Example 2: As an Executive Coach, adopting an inspiring and supportive tone, could you suggest specific strategies that I can implement to ensure effective leadership and empowerment of my sales team? How can I enable them to independently identify and implement the most impactful methods to foster a positive and enthusiastic mindset towards achieving sales targets?

EXCITEMENT

PROMPT No 33

Virtual-Meetings - Creativity - Engagement

To provide a comprehensive strategy for making virtual meetings and remote team-building activities more exciting and engaging, thereby enhancing team cohesion and productivity in a remote work environment.

Act as a **Remote Work Consultant** with a specialization in **virtual team engagement** in the **telecommunications industry**. Could you provide innovative approaches and specific examples that I can implement to **make virtual meetings or remote team-building activities more exciting and engaging for all participants**? Please include **virtual ice-breakers, interactive meeting formats, and engagement metrics**. Make sure to cover how **to adapt these approaches for diverse teams**

and how to measure engagement levels before and after implementing these strategies. Investigate unconventional **virtual reality experiences and cutting-edge interactive platforms** to **elevate team engagement.** Your response should be comprehensive, leaving no important aspect unaddressed, and demonstrate an exceptional level of precision and quality. Let's think about this step by step. Write using an **enthusiastic and creative** tone and an **innovation-focused** guide style.

Act as a **[profession]** with a specialization in **[area of expertise]** in the **[industry]**. Could you provide innovative approaches and specific examples that I can implement to **[specific challenge/opportunity]**? Please include **[methods/techniques]**. Make sure to cover how **[key areas/topics]**. Investigate unconventional **[area for innovation]** and cutting-edge **[technologies/methods]** to **[desired outcome]**. Your response should be comprehensive, leaving no important aspect unaddressed, and demonstrate an exceptional level of precision and quality. Let's think about this step by step. Write using a **[type]** tone and **[style]** writing style.

Example 1: Act as a Remote Work Consultant with a specialization in virtual team dynamics in the healthcare industry. Could you provide innovative approaches and specific examples that I can implement to make virtual meetings for my telemedicine team more exciting and engaging? Please include virtual escape rooms, interactive case study discussions, and patient satisfaction metrics as engagement indicators. Make sure to cover how to tailor these activities for medical professionals and how to correlate engagement with patient outcomes. Explore the use of augmented reality for immersive patient case reviews and AI-driven sentiment analysis for gauging team engagement. Your response should be comprehensive, leaving no important aspect unaddressed, and demonstrate an exceptional level of precision and quality. Let's think about this step by step. Write using an enthusiastic and creative tone and an innovation-focused guide style.

Example 2: Act as a Remote Work Consultant with a specialization in virtual collaboration tools in the software development industry. Could you provide innovative approaches and specific examples that I can implement to make sprint planning meetings for my remote development team more exciting and engaging? Please include gamified task assignments, interactive sprint boards, and velocity metrics. Make sure to cover how to adapt these approaches for cross-functional teams and how to measure engagement through sprint completion rates. Delve into the use of holographic stand-ups and blockchain-based task tracking for transparent and engaging workflows. Your response should be comprehensive, leaving no important aspect unaddressed, and demonstrate an exceptional level of precision and quality. Let's think about this step by step. Write using an enthusiastic and creative tone and an innovation-focused guide style.

PROMPT No 34

Efficiency - Precision - Time-Management

To gain insights on how professionals can effectively manage the trade-off between working quickly and efficiently, while also maintaining a high level of precision and accuracy in their tasks.

As a **Time Management Expert**, adopting a **practical and insightful tone**, could you provide strategies or techniques that **investment professionals** can use to effectively balance the need for **speed and efficiency** with the importance of **thoroughness and accuracy** in their work?

As a [profession], adopting a [tone of voice], could you provide strategies or techniques that [professionals/individuals/Role] can use to effectively balance the need for [contextual challenge/opportunity] with the importance of [contextual challenge/opportunity] in their work?

Example 1: As a Productivity Coach, adopting a motivational and clear tone, could you provide strategies that project managers can use to effectively balance the need for speed and efficiency with the importance of thoroughness and accuracy in their project execution?

Example 2: As a Business Efficiency Consultant, adopting a professional and solution-oriented tone, could you provide techniques that sales professionals can use to effectively balance the need for quick client responses with the importance of providing accurate and detailed information in their communication?

FEAR

PROMPT No 35

Transparency - Empowerment - HR

To gain insights on specific strategies or approaches that have proven to be successful in fostering an environment where team members feel comfortable and empowered to express their concerns about the workplace culture or their work overall, encouraging open and honest communication.

As a **Human Resources Consultant**, adopting an **empathetic and understanding tone**, could you provide me with specific strategies or approaches that have proven to be successful in fostering an environment where **team members** feel comfortable and empowered to express their concerns about **the workplace culture or their work overall**? This is particularly relevant given the goal of **encouraging open and honest communication within the team.**

As a [profession], adopting a [tone of voice], could you provide me with specific strategies or approaches that have proven to be successful in fostering an environment where [my/their] [team/group/department] feel comfortable and empowered to express their concerns about

[contextual challenge/opportunity]? This is particularly relevant given the goal of **[desired outcome]**.

Example 1: As a Leadership Development Facilitator, adopting a respectful and supportive tone, could you provide me with specific strategies that have proven to be successful in fostering an environment where engineering team members feel comfortable and empowered to express their concerns about the engineering-related responsibilities? This is particularly relevant given the goal of encouraging open and honest communication within the team.

Example 2: As a Team Coach, adopting a patient and understanding tone, could you provide me with specific approaches that have proven to be successful in fostering an environment where my legal team feels comfortable and empowered to express their concerns about their team culture? This is particularly relevant given the goal of encouraging open and honest communication within the legal team.

PROMPT No 36

Empowerment - Ambition - Anxiety

To gain specific strategies for creating a nurturing and empowering atmosphere that motivates team members to wholeheartedly pursue ambitious objectives, even in the face of their own apprehensions and anxieties.

As a **Leadership Development Consultant**, adopting a **supportive and encouraging tone**, could you provide specific strategies that **I** can implement to create a **nurturing and empowering atmosphere that motivates my team members to wholeheartedly pursue ambitious objectives**, even when they are faced with their own **apprehensions and anxieties**?

As a **[profession]**, adopting a **[tone of voice]**, could you provide specific strategies that **[I/Name/Role]** can implement to create a **[desired outcome]**, even when they are faced with their own **[contextual challenge/opportunity]**?

Example 1: As a Team Coach, adopting a motivating and positive tone, could you provide specific strategies that a sustainability manager can implement to create a nurturing and empowering atmosphere that motivates their sustainability team to wholeheartedly pursue ambitious objectives, even when they are faced with their own apprehensions and anxieties?

Example 2: As an Executive Coach, adopting an inspiring and supportive tone, could you provide specific strategies that I can implement to create a nurturing and empowering atmosphere that motivates my ethics and compliance team to wholeheartedly pursue ambitious objectives, even when they are faced with their own apprehensions and anxieties?

PROMPT No 37

Tags

Motivation - Confidence - Leadership

Goal

To gain specific strategies and practices that can be implemented to create a work environment that effectively supports and motivates team members to overcome their fears and gain confidence in their skills and capabilities.

Prompt

As a **Leadership Development Consultant**, adopting an **encouraging and supportive tone**, could you provide specific strategies and practices that **I** can implement to create a work environment that effectively supports and motivates **my team members** to overcome their fears and gain confidence in their skills and capabilities?

Formula

As a **[profession]**, adopting a **[tone of voice]**, could you provide specific strategies and practices that **[I/Name/Role]** can implement to create a work environment that effectively supports and motivates **[my/their]** **[team/group/department]** to overcome their fears and gain confidence in their skills and capabilities?

Examples

Example 1: As a Team Coach, adopting a motivating and positive tone, could you provide specific strategies and practices that a branding manager can implement to create a work environment that effectively supports and motivates their branding team to overcome their fears and gain confidence in their skills and capabilities?

Example 2: As an Executive Coach, adopting an inspiring and supportive tone, could you provide specific strategies and practices that I can implement to create a work environment that effectively supports and motivates my mergers and acquisitions team to overcome their fears and gain confidence in their skills and capabilities?

FEELINGS

PROMPT No 38

Tags

Well-being - Productivity - Workplace

Goal

To gain specific strategies or techniques that can be utilized to significantly improve a team's comprehension of the various factors that impact their emotions and overall well-being, fostering a healthier and more productive work environment.

As a **Workplace Wellness Consultant**, adopting a **supportive and empathetic tone**, could you provide specific strategies or techniques that can be utilized to significantly improve my **team's** comprehension of the various factors that **impact their emotions and overall well-being**? This is particularly relevant given the goal of **fostering a healthier and more productive work environment**.

As a [profession], adopting a [tone of voice], could you provide specific strategies or techniques that can be utilized to significantly improve [my/their] [team/group/department]'s comprehension of the various factors that [contextual challenge/opportunity]? This is particularly relevant given the goal of [desired outcome].

Example 1:   As a Mental Health at Work Consultant, adopting a compassionate and understanding tone, could you provide specific strategies or techniques that can be utilized to significantly improve a department's comprehension of the various factors that impact their stress levels and overall well-being? This is particularly relevant given the goal of fostering a healthier and more productive work environment.

Example 2:   As a Corporate Wellness Coach, adopting a motivational and inspiring tone, could you provide specific strategies or techniques that can be utilized to significantly improve my sales team's comprehension of the various factors that impact their emotional health and overall well-being? This is particularly relevant given the goal of fostering a healthier and more productive sales environment.

PROMPT No 39

Self-Reflection - Emotions - Unconscious

To gain specific self-reflection exercises that can assist team members in effectively identifying and exploring their unconscious emotions and attitudes towards their work.

As a **Leadership Development Consultant**, adopting an **empathetic and understanding tone**, could you suggest specific **self-reflection exercises** that **my team members** can engage in to **effectively identify and explore their unconscious emotions and attitudes towards their work**?

As a [profession], adopting a [tone of voice], could you suggest specific [contextual challenge/opportunity] that [my/their] [team/group/department] can engage in to [desired outcome]?

Example 1: As a Team Coach, adopting a supportive and patient tone, could you suggest specific self-reflection exercises that a design team can engage in to effectively identify and explore their unconscious emotions and attitudes towards their design work?

Example 2: As a Performance Management Specialist, adopting a respectful and encouraging tone, could you suggest specific self-reflection exercises that my government affairs team can engage in to effectively identify and explore their unconscious emotions and attitudes towards their work with governmental organizations?

PROMPT No 40

Impact - Performance - Management

To gain specific strategies, methods, or approaches to comprehensively assess and fully comprehend the true impact and ramifications of an issue or problem, which has originated from senior management, on a team's performance, dynamics, and overall well-being.

As a **Management Consultant**, adopting a **solution-oriented tone**, could you provide detailed strategies, methods, or approaches that **I** can employ to **comprehensively assess and fully comprehend the true impact and ramifications of an issue or problem**, which has originated from **senior management**, on my **team**'s performance, dynamics, and overall well-being?

As a [profession], adopting a [tone of voice], could you provide detailed strategies, methods, or approaches that [I/Name/Role] can employ to [desired outcome], which has originated from [contextual challenge/opportunity], on [my/their] [team/group/department]'s performance, dynamics, and overall well-being?

Example 1: As a Business Analyst, adopting a data-driven tone, could you provide detailed strategies, methods, or approaches that a department head can employ to comprehensively assess and fully comprehend the true impact and ramifications of an issue or problem, which has originated from a recent policy change, on their faculty's performance, dynamics, and overall well-being?

Example 2: As a Human Resources (HR) Consultant, adopting a empathetic and professional tone, could you provide detailed strategies, methods, or approaches that I can employ to comprehensively assess and fully comprehend the true impact and ramifications of an issue or problem, which has originated from a recent restructuring, on my project team's performance, dynamics, and overall well-being?

FLOW

PROMPT No 41

Obstacles - Flow - Strategies

To understand potential obstacles that can prevent team members from achieving a state of 'flow' and to learn strategies or actions that can be employed to effectively tackle these challenges and promote a conducive environment for achieving 'flow'.

As a **Leadership Development Consultant**, adopting a **solution-oriented tone**, could you enlighten me on the specific obstacles or difficulties that can hinder **my team members** from attaining **a state of 'flow'**? Additionally, what strategies or actions can I employ to effectively tackle these challenges and promote a conducive environment for achieving 'flow'?

As a **[profession]**, adopting a **[tone of voice]**, could you enlighten me on the specific obstacles or difficulties that can hinder **[my/their]** **[team/group/department]** from attaining **[contextual challenge/opportunity]**? Additionally, what strategies or actions can **[I/Name/Role]** employ to effectively tackle these challenges and promote **[desired outcome]**?

Example 1: As a Performance Coach, adopting a practical and insightful tone, could you enlighten me on the specific obstacles or difficulties that can hinder my facilities management team from attaining a state of 'flow'? Additionally, what strategies or actions can I employ to effectively tackle these challenges and promote a conducive environment for achieving 'flow'?

Example 2: As a Team Development Specialist, adopting a constructive and encouraging tone, could you enlighten a customer support team manager on the specific obstacles or difficulties that can hinder their customer support team from attaining a state of 'flow'? Additionally, what strategies or actions can they employ to effectively tackle these challenges and promote a conducive environment for achieving 'flow'?

PROMPT No 42

Optimal-Self - Performance - Problem-Solving

To gain insights on methods to help a team access their optimal self, enhancing their performance and problem-solving capabilities.

In the context of **managing daily responsibilities and problems**, as a **Performance Coach** and in an **empowering and motivating tone**, could you outline the methods **I** could use to help **my team** access their optimal self?

In the context of **[contextual challenge/opportunity]**, as a **[profession]** and in a **[tone of voice]**, could you outline the methods **[I/Name/Role]** could use to help **[my/their]** **[team/group/department]** access their optimal self when dealing with **[responsibilities/problems/specific area]**?

Example 1: In the context of managing complex project tasks, as a Team Coach and in an encouraging and supportive tone, could you outline the methods a project manager could use to help their team access their optimal self?

Example 2: As a Leadership Development Consultant, in an inspiring and energetic tone, could you outline the methods I could use to help my accounting team access their optimal self when dealing with customer relations, especially in the context of managing challenging customer interactions?

FULFILLMENT

PROMPT No 43

Cohesion - Development - Realization

To gain insights on the steps and items to consider when identifying factors that hinder a team from becoming more fully realized, enhancing their development and cohesion.

Given the goal of **developing a more fully realized team**, as an **Organizational Development Consultant** and in a **solution-oriented tone**, could you confirm the steps and items to consider when trying to identify the factors that hinder **my team** from **achieving this**?

Given the goal of **[contextual challenge/opportunity]**, as a **[profession]** and in a **[tone of voice]**, could you confirm the steps and items to consider when trying to identify the factors that hinder **[I/Name/Role]'s** **[team/group/department]** from **[desired outcome]**?

Example 1: Given the goal of developing a more cohesive marketing team, as a Team Coach and in a clear and concise tone, could you confirm the steps and items a marketing manager should consider when trying to identify the factors that hinder their team from becoming more fully realized?

Example 2: As a Leadership Development Facilitator, in a respectful and patient tone, could you confirm the steps and items to consider when trying to identify the factors that hinder my sales team from becoming a more fully realized team, especially given the goal of improving team performance?

GOALS

Tags

Values - Integration - Aspirations

Goal

To gain insights on how leaders can effectively align their personal values, goals, and aspirations with their professional duties and obligations, ensuring that their personal purpose is integrated into their professional roles and responsibilities.

Prompt

As a **Leadership Development Consultant**, adopting an **insightful and strategic tone**, could you provide a comprehensive and detailed explanation of the strategies that **leaders** can employ to effectively align **their personal values, goals, and aspirations** with **their professional duties and obligations**? This is particularly relevant given the goal of **integrating personal purpose into professional roles and responsibilities**.

Formula

As a **[profession]**, adopting a **[tone of voice]**, could you provide a comprehensive and detailed explanation of the strategies that **[I/Name/Role]** can employ to effectively align **[contextual challenge/opportunity]** with **[contextual challenge/opportunity]**? This is particularly relevant given the goal of **[desired outcome]**.

Examples

Example 1: As a Career Coach, adopting a supportive and strategic tone, could you provide a comprehensive and detailed explanation of the strategies that a mid-career professional can employ to effectively align their personal values, goals, and aspirations with their professional duties and obligations? This is particularly relevant given the goal of integrating personal purpose into professional roles and responsibilities.

Example 2: As an Executive Coach, adopting a thoughtful and strategic tone, could you provide a comprehensive and detailed explanation of the strategies that I, as a CEO, can employ to effectively align my personal values, goals, and aspirations with my professional duties and obligations? This is particularly relevant given the goal of integrating personal purpose into my professional role and responsibilities.

Tags

Empowerment - Leadership - Strategies

Goal

To gain detailed insights on actions and strategies a team leader can implement to support and empower team members in leveraging their strengths towards achieving collective goals, enhancing team performance and success.

Prompt

As a **Leadership Coach**, in an **empowering and supportive tone**, could you explain in detail the actions and strategies that **I, as a team leader**, can implement to effectively support and empower **my team members** to leverage their individual strengths and abilities towards achieving our **collective goals**?

Formula

As a [profession], in a [tone of voice], could you explain in detail the actions and strategies that [I/Name/Role], as a [specific role], can implement to effectively support and empower [my/their] [team/group/department] members to leverage their individual strengths and abilities towards achieving our [specific goal/outcome]?

Examples

Example 1: As a Team Coach, in an encouraging and motivational tone, could you explain in detail the actions and strategies that a project manager can implement to effectively support and empower their project team members to leverage their individual strengths and abilities towards achieving project completion on time?

Example 2: In an inspirational and enthusiastic tone, could you explain in detail the actions and strategies that I, as a sales team leader, can implement to effectively support and empower my sales team members to leverage their individual strengths and abilities towards achieving our quarterly sales targets? As a Sales Performance Coach, your insights would be highly valuable.

PROMPT No 46

Tags

Resources - Development - Support

Goal

To gain insights on the specific resources, tools, and support colleagues require at each stage of their professional development, enhancing their ability to achieve their desired objectives.

Prompt

Considering the importance of providing adequate resources and support for professional development, as a **Talent Development Specialist** and in a **solution-oriented and respectful tone**, could you identify what specific resources, tools, and support **my colleagues** require at each stage of their professional development in order to successfully achieve their desired objectives?

Formula

Considering the importance of **[contextual challenge/opportunity]**, as a **[profession]** and in a **[tone of voice]**, could you identify what specific resources, tools, and support **[I/Name/Role]'s [colleagues/team/group/department]** require at each stage of their **[specific area]** in order to successfully achieve their **[desired outcome]**?

Examples

Example 1: Considering the importance of providing adequate resources and support for career progression, as a Career Coach and in a supportive and patient tone, could you identify what specific resources, tools, and support my colleagues in the marketing department require at each stage of their career development in order to successfully achieve their promotion goals?

Example 2: As a Human Resources Consultant, in a clear and concise tone, could you identify what specific resources, tools, and support my colleagues in the research and development team require at each stage of their skill development in order to successfully achieve their innovation objectives? This advice is particularly relevant considering the importance of continuous learning in a rapidly evolving tech industry.

PROMPT No 47

Tags

Self-Improvement - Career - Conflict

Goal

To gain insights on specific steps or actions to plan for advancing personal growth and development, enhancing self-improvement and goal achievement.

Prompt

As a **Career Coach**, in an **encouraging and supportive tone**, could you describe in detail what specific steps or actions **someone** should plan to take in order to advance their personal growth and development about **learning to deal with conflict**? This advice is sought particularly considering the importance of continuous learning in today's fast-paced professional environment.

Formula

As a **[profession]**, in a **[tone of voice]**, could you describe in detail what specific steps or actions **[someone/I/Name/Role]** should plan to take in order to advance their **[desired outcome]** about **[Topic]**? This advice is sought particularly considering the importance of **[contextual challenge/opportunity]**.

Examples

HABITS

PROMPT No 48

Tags

Quality - Efficiency - Error-Reduction

Goal

To identify and implement strategies to reduce errors or miscalculations within a team's workflow, thereby enhancing accuracy, efficiency, and overall performance. The ultimate aim is to cultivate a culture of excellence, attention to detail, and continuous improvement that ensures the delivery of high-quality work.

Prompt

Act as a **Quality Assurance Specialist** specializing in the **manufacturing industry**. Could you delineate strategies that my team could consider implementing to **significantly reduce errors or miscalculations in their daily operations**? This reduction is crucial for **maintaining product quality, improving efficiency, safeguarding compliance, and building customer trust**. Please present a comprehensive plan, encompassing **training initiatives, process refinement, technology solutions, monitoring mechanisms, and feedback loops**. Let's examine this **step by step**. Write using an **authoritative** tone and **clear** writing style.

Formula

Act as a **[profession]** specializing in the **[industry]**. Could you delineate strategies that my team could consider implementing to **[contextual challenge/opportunity]**? This reduction is crucial for **[desired outcome]**. Please present a comprehensive plan, encompassing **[specific components or methods]**. Let's examine this **[methodically/step by step/one piece at a time]**. Write using a **[type]** tone and **[style]** writing style.

Examples

Example 1: Act as a Risk Management Consultant specializing in the finance industry. Could you delineate strategies that my investment team could consider implementing to minimize errors or miscalculations in their financial analysis? This minimization is essential for mitigating risks, enhancing investment returns, maintaining regulatory compliance, and fostering client confidence. Please offer a robust approach, including specialized training, analytical tools, validation protocols, ongoing monitoring, and responsive feedback systems. Let's dissect this carefully. Write using a persuasive tone and analytical writing style.

Example 2:   Act as a Process Improvement Expert specializing in the software development industry. Could you delineate strategies that my development team could consider implementing to decrease bugs or miscalculations in their coding? This improvement is vital for delivering reliable software, improving user experience, accelerating development cycles, and strengthening brand reputation. Please craft a multifaceted solution, integrating coding standards, automated testing, peer reviews, continuous integration, and iterative feedback mechanisms. Let's approach this methodically. Write using an instructive tone and engaging writing style.

PROMPT No 49

Productivity - SocialMedia - Distractions

To gain insights on specific measures to overcome the unhealthy tendency of being distracted by social media during work hours, enhancing work productivity.

Given the challenge of **social media distractions during work hours**, as a **Performance Coach** and in a **clear and concise tone**, could you suggest specific measures that can be taken to overcome this **unhealthy tendency** with the aim of **enhancing work productivity**?

Given the challenge of **[contextual challenge/opportunity]**, as a **[profession]** and in a **[tone of voice]**, could you suggest specific measures that can be taken to overcome **[issue]** with the aim of **[desired outcome]**?

Example 1: Given the challenge of social media distractions in a digital marketing team, as a Team Coach and in a solution-oriented tone, could you suggest specific measures that a team leader can take to overcome this unhealthy tendency with the aim of enhancing team productivity?

Example 2: As a Human Resources Consultant, in a professional and respectful tone, could you suggest specific measures that can be taken to overcome the unhealthy tendency of being distracted by social media during work hours, with the aim of enhancing work productivity? This advice is particularly relevant given the challenge of maintaining focus in a remote work environment.

LEARNING

PROMPT No 50

Reflection - Growth - Improvement

To provide guidance and insights on reflecting and learning from recent experiences. It aims to empower teams to identify key takeaways, learn from them, and integrate these learnings into future actions and decisions.

Act as a **Leadership Development Consultant** specializing in the **event planning industry**. What are some **tips I could share with my team to reflect on and learn from the key takeaways from a recent experience**? This reflection is crucial for **personal and professional growth, fostering a culture of continuous improvement and resilience**. Ensuring that your response is thorough, precise, and of the highest quality possible. Let's analyze this piece by piece. Write using a **motivational** tone and **conversational** writing style.

Act as a **[profession]** specializing in the **[industry]**. What are some **[contextual challenge/opportunity]**? This reflection is crucial for **[desired outcome]**. Ensuring that your response is thorough, precise, and of the highest quality possible. Let's analyze this piece by piece. Write using a **[type]** tone and **[style]** writing style.

Example 1: Act as a Team Coach specializing in the sales industry, what guidance could I impart to my team to reflect on and glean insights from their recent sales pitches? Such reflection is instrumental in refining our approach, enhancing customer relationships, and driving sales performance. Let's dissect this carefully. Write using an enthusiastic tone and informative writing style.

Example 2: Act as an Organizational Psychologist specializing in the manufacturing industry, what advice could I offer my team to analyze and learn from recent changes in our production process? Understanding and learning from this experience is vital to continuous improvement, efficiency, and innovation within our operations. Let's think about this step by step. Write using an authoritative tone and technical writing style.

PROMPT No 51

Improvement - Recognition - Learning

To gain specific actions or methods that can be employed to successfully improve a team's understanding and recognition of the areas that were not successful or did not achieve the desired outcomes, fostering a culture of continuous learning and improvement.

As a **Performance Coach**, adopting a **constructive and supportive tone**, could you provide specific actions or methods that **I** can employ to successfully improve **my team's** understanding and recognition of the areas that were not successful or did not achieve the desired outcomes? This is particularly relevant given the goal of **fostering a culture of continuous learning and improvement**.

As a **[profession]**, adopting a **[tone of voice]**, could you provide specific actions or methods that **[I/Name/Role]** can employ to successfully improve **[my/their]** **[team/group/department]'s** understanding and recognition of [contextual challenge/opportunity]? This is particularly relevant given the goal of [desired outcome].

Example 1: As a Business Coach, adopting a constructive and supportive tone, could you provide specific actions or methods that a department head can employ to successfully improve their marketing team's understanding and recognition of the areas that were not successful or did not achieve the desired outcomes? This is particularly relevant given the goal of fostering a culture of continuous learning and improvement within the marketing department.

Example 2: As a Leadership Trainer, adopting a constructive and supportive tone, could you provide specific actions or methods that I can employ to successfully improve my project team's understanding and recognition of the areas that were not successful or did not achieve the desired outcomes? This is particularly relevant given the goal of fostering a culture of continuous learning and improvement within the project team.

PROMPT No 52

Tags

Growth - Criteria - Evaluation

Goal

To guide an individual in identifying and evaluating the various criteria that will influence their selection of areas for personal or professional growth. This includes understanding one's current strengths and weaknesses, values, career or life objectives, opportunities available, and other relevant factors

Prompt

Act as a **Personal Development Coach** specializing in the **environmental assessment industry**. What are the distinct criteria or factors I **should weigh and assess to pinpoint the domains where I could focus on growing either professionally or personally**? How do these aspects interplay with **my long-term objectives, values, and current capabilities**? Respond to each question separately. Explore unconventional solutions and alternative perspectives. Let's dissect this carefully. Write using an **insightful** tone and **informative** writing style.

Formula

Act as a **[profession]** specializing in the **[industry]**. What are the distinct criteria or factors I **[contextual challenge/opportunity]**? How do these aspects interplay with **[contextual challenge/opportunity]**? Respond to each question separately. Explore unconventional solutions and alternative perspectives. Let's dissect this carefully. Write using a **[type]** tone and **[style]** writing style.

Examples

Example 1: Act as a Career Development Coach specializing in the technology industry. What are the vital criteria I should weigh to identify the most promising fields where I could enhance my professional capabilities? How do these elements align with my career aspirations, technological trends, and current skill set? Respond to each question separately. Investigate unexpected avenues and creative pathways. Let's analyze this piece by piece. Write using an enthusiastic tone and engaging writing style.

Example 2: Act as a Life Coach specializing in personal growth. What are the various factors I need to consider to select the areas where I should focus on personal development and self-improvement? How do these aspects connect with my life's goals, personal values, and existing strengths or weaknesses? Respond to each question separately. Discover rare insights and pioneering ideas. Let's unpack this topic. Write using a motivational tone and creative writing style.

PROMPT No 53

Tags

Leadership - Wellbeing - Collaboration

Goal

To identify critical variables that can help a leader ensure the wellbeing and happiness of their team in a business environment. These variables might include factors related to work-life balance, job satisfaction, mental and physical health, collaboration, and motivation. Understanding and monitoring these variables can enable the team leader to create a supportive and fulfilling workplace.

Prompt

Act as a **Leadership Development Consultant** specializing in the **banking industry**. What are the **essential** variables that I should **observe** when **working** with my **team** to **ensure** their **well-being**? How can I **recognize** signs of **stress**, and what **tools** can I implement to promote a **healthy** work **environment**? What are some **real-world examples** that have been **effective** in **maintaining team** well-being? Respond separately to each question. Explore unconventional solutions and alternative perspectives. Let's take this one step at a time. Write using an **empathetic** tone and **constructive** writing style.

Formula

Act as a **[profession]** specializing in the **[industry]**. What are the **[essential/critical/key]** variables that I should **[observe/monitor/consider]** when **[working/engaging/collaborating]** with my **[team/staff/employees]** to **[ensure/maintain/guarantee]** their **[wellbeing/happiness/satisfaction]**? How can I **[recognize/identify/detect]** **[signs/symptoms/indicators]** of **[stress/burnout/dissatisfaction]**, and what **[tools/strategies/methods]** can I **[implement/employ/use]** to **[promote/support/create]** a **[healthy/motivating/positive]** work **[environment/atmosphere/culture]**? What are some **[real-world/practical/actual]** **[examples/cases/instances]** **[best practices/guidelines/standards]** that have been **[effective/successful/proven]** in **[maintaining/supporting/upholding]** **[team/group/staff]** wellbeing? Respond separately to each question. Explore unconventional solutions and alternative perspectives. Let's take this one step at a time. Write using a **[type]** tone and **[style]** writing style.

Examples

Example 1: Act as an Employee Engagement Consultant specializing in the tech industry, what are the key variables such as communication, work-life balance, job satisfaction, and peer relationships that I should monitor when engaging with my team to ensure their overall happiness? How can regular one-on-one meetings, anonymous surveys, and team-building activities be utilized to detect and address potential issues? What are some successful tech companies that have implemented these practices to foster a healthy work environment? Respond separately to each question. Let's consider each facet of this topic. Unearth hidden gems and non-traditional methods. Write using an enthusiastic tone and informative writing style.

Example 2: Act as a Performance Coach specializing in the banking industry, what are the essential factors like mental health support, recognition, clear expectations, and growth opportunities that I should consider when working with my team to maintain their well-being? How can tools such as performance reviews, mental health programs, and open-door policies help in promoting a satisfying work experience? What are some well-regarded financial institutions that prioritize employee well-being, and how have they achieved this? Respond separately to each question. Discover rare insights and pioneering ideas. Let's take this one step at a time. Write using a professional tone and analytical writing style.

PROMPT No 54

Tags
CriticalReview - Solutions - ActionableInsights

Goal
To create an open and psychologically safe environment for the team to critically examine and discuss the least beneficial aspects of their work. The objective is to collectively identify these aspects, explore their root causes, and brainstorm actionable solutions, all while avoiding blame or discouragement.

Prompt
Act as an **Organizational Behavior Expert** specializing in **critical review and feedback systems** for the **health care industry**. Could you provide a **well-rounded guide** on how **to initiate and facilitate a team discussion about the least beneficial aspects of their work?** I am particularly interested in **strategies that promote openness and critical thinking, as well as techniques for turning identified issues into actionable insights.** The guide should be divided into **stages: preparation, execution, and follow-up.** Deliver an all-inclusive and extensive output. Let's systematically explore each facet.   Write using a **constructive** tone and a **solutions-focused** writing style.

Formula
Act as a **[profession]** specializing in **[expertise/specialization]** for the **[industry]**. Could you provide a **[comprehensive type of resource/tool]** on how to **[specific objective]**? I am particularly interested in **[specific methods/techniques/goals]**. The guide should be divided into **[specific stages/sections]**. Deliver an all-inclusive and extensive output. Let's systematically explore each

facet. Propose a comprehensive and elaborate response. Let's carefully evaluate each aspect. Write using a **[type]** tone and **[style]** writing style.

Examples

Example 1: Act as a Leadership Coach specializing in conflict resolution. Could you outline a structured conversation guide aimed at discussing the least effective practices within the team? I want to ensure the conversation remains objective and non-confrontational. Include a section on framing the conversation, question prompts, and a roadmap for implementing solutions. Express unusual guidance and neglected opportunities. Let's break this down into its constituent parts. Write using a diplomatic tone and a process-oriented writing style.

Example 2: Act as a Business Analyst specializing in operational efficiency. Could you offer a data-driven approach to facilitate a team discussion about underperforming aspects of their roles? I am particularly keen on incorporating metrics and KPIs to keep the discussion grounded in facts. Include data collection methods, analytical frameworks, and a strategy for ongoing measurement and improvement. Suggest offbeat approaches and hidden gems. Let's take this one step at a time. Write using an analytical tone and a data-backed writing style.

PROMPT No 55

Tags

Preparation - Conversation - Learning

Goal

To gain insights on practical strategies or steps to prepare for an effective conversation with the team about valuable lessons they've learned from challenging professional experiences, fostering a culture of shared learning and growth.

Prompt

As an **Executive Coach**, adopting an **empathetic and encouraging tone**, could you outline the specific strategies or steps that I can take to ensure that I am fully prepared to engage in a meaningful and effective conversation with my team regarding the valuable lessons they have gained from a challenging experience in their professional lives? This is particularly pertinent in fostering a culture of shared learning and growth.

Formula

As a **[profession]**, adopting a **[tone of voice]**, could you outline the specific strategies or steps that **[team/group/department]** can take to ensure that I am fully prepared **[contextual challenge/opportunity]**? This is particularly pertinent in fostering **[desired outcome]**.

Examples

Example 1: As a Team Coach, adopting a supportive and encouraging tone, could you outline the specific strategies or steps that I can take to ensure that I am fully prepared to engage in a meaningful and effective conversation with my project team regarding the valuable lessons they have gained from a challenging project? This is particularly pertinent in fostering a culture of shared learning and growth within the project team.

Example 2: As a Leadership Development Consultant, adopting a constructive and empathetic tone, could you outline the specific strategies or steps that a manager can take to ensure that they are fully prepared to engage in a meaningful and effective conversation with their department regarding the valuable lessons they have gained from a rewarding period in their professional lives? This is particularly pertinent in fostering a culture of shared learning and growth within the department.

PROMPT No 56

Tags

Reflection - Improvement - Strategy

Goal

To gain insights on specific strategies or methods to encourage a team to reflect on a past situation where their actions could have been improved, fostering reflective learning and continuous improvement.

Prompt

Considering the importance of **reflective learning for continuous improvement**, as a **Leadership Coach** and in an **empathetic and respectful tone**, could you suggest specific strategies or methods **I** can implement with **my team** to **encourage them to reflect on a past situation where their actions could have been improved**?

Formula

Considering the importance of **[contextual challenge/opportunity]**, as a **[profession]** and in a **[tone of voice]**, could you suggest specific strategies or methods **[I/Name/Role]** can implement with **[my/their]** **[team/group/department]** to **[desired outcome]**?

Examples

Example 1: Considering the importance of reflective learning for continuous improvement in a healthcare setting, as a Team Coach and in a patient and supportive tone, could you suggest specific strategies or methods a healthcare manager can implement with their team to encourage them to reflect on a past situation where their actions could have been improved?

Example 2: As a Performance Coach, in an encouraging and considerate tone, could you suggest specific strategies or methods I can implement with my customer service team to encourage them to reflect on a past situation where their actions could have been improved? This advice is particularly relevant considering the importance of reflective learning for continuous improvement in customer service.

PROMPT No 57

Tags
Project-Management - Strategy - Progress

Goal
To gain insights on specific strategies or methods to facilitate the progress of a project being undertaken by a team, enhancing project management and team performance.

Prompt
In the context of **facilitating the progress of a project**, as a **Project Management Consultant** and in a **clear and concise tone**, could you suggest specific strategies or methods **I** can implement with **my team**?

Formula
In the context of **[contextual challenge/opportunity]**, as a **[profession]** and in a **[tone of voice]**, could you suggest specific strategies or methods **[I/Name/Role]** can implement with **[my/their]** **[team/group/department]**?

Examples
Example 1: In the context of facilitating the progress of a software development project, as an IT Project Manager and in a solution-oriented and professional tone, could you suggest specific strategies or methods a team leader can implement with their team?
Example 2: As a Management Consultant, in a supportive and clear tone, could you suggest specific strategies or methods I can implement with my marketing team to facilitate the progress of our upcoming product launch project? This advice is particularly relevant in the context of ensuring a successful product launch in a competitive market.

PROMPT No 58

Tags
Public-Speaking - Professional-Development - Confidence

Goal
To help you in enhancing your public speaking skills. It covers all aspects of public speaking, from understanding the audience to crafting the message, using effective body language, managing anxiety, utilizing visual aids, and continuous improvement through feedback and practice.

Prompt
Act as a **Professional Development and Communication Coach** specializing in the **technology industry**. **Public speaking** is an **essential** skill for **leaders**. How can **I develop my** public speaking skills to **convey ideas** with **confidence**? Provide a **comprehensive** guide that includes **understanding** the **audience's needs, crafting compelling content, utilizing storytelling, body language, vocal variety,**

visual aids, handling questions, managing anxiety, and creating opportunities for feedback and continuous practice. Include actionable steps, tools, resources, and examples of how these strategies can be applied in various professional contexts. Respond separately to each question. Provide exhaustive and all-encompassing responses. Let's break this down into manageable parts. Write using a confident tone and assertive writing style.

Act as a [profession] specializing in the [industry]. [public speaking/presentation/communication] is a [crucial/essential/vital] skill for [professionals/leaders/managers/employees]. How can [individual/professional/speaker] [develop/refine/enhance] [my/their] public speaking skills to [convey/communicate/present] [ideas/messages/information] with [confidence/clarity/impact]? Provide a [comprehensive/thorough/complete] guide that includes [understanding/analyzing/assessing] the [audience's needs/preferences], [crafting/composing/creating] [compelling/engaging/effective] [content/message/speech], [utilizing/employing/leveraging] [storytelling/metaphors/anecdotes], [body language/gestures/facial expressions], [vocal variety/tone/pacing], [visual aids/slides/props], [handling/responding to/questions], [managing/overcoming/reducing] [anxiety/nervousness/fear], and [creating/seeking/finding] [opportunities/venues/channels] for [feedback/evaluation/practice]. Include [actionable steps/tips/strategies], [tools/resources/guides], and [examples/scenarios/case studies] of how these [strategies/techniques/methods] can be [applied/implemented/used] in [various/different/multiple] [professional contexts/settings/environments]. Respond separately to each question. Provide exhaustive and all-encompassing responses. Let's break this down into manageable parts. Write using a [type] tone and [style] writing style.

Example 1: Act as a Leadership Communication Coach in the technology industry, where conveying complex ideas simply is crucial. How can a tech executive develop their public speaking skills to effectively present technical information to non-technical stakeholders? Provide a comprehensive guide that includes translating technical jargon into layman's terms, storytelling to create relatability, using visual aids for clarity, managing Q&A sessions, and continuous practice with diverse audiences. Include examples and scenarios specific to the technology field. Respond separately to each question. Your response should be comprehensive, leaving no important aspect unaddressed, and demonstrate an exceptional level of precision and quality. Let's break this down into manageable parts. Write using an empathetic tone and understanding writing style.

Example 2: Act as a Sales Presentation Expert in the pharmaceutical industry, where persuading clients and regulators is a core part of the job. How can a pharmaceutical sales representative refine their public speaking skills to make compelling pitches and presentations? Provide a detailed guide that includes understanding the audience's concerns, crafting persuasive arguments, using body language and vocal variety for emphasis, handling objections, and utilizing feedback for continuous improvement. Include case studies and tools relevant to the pharmaceutical sales environment. Respond separately to each question. Propose comprehensive and elaborate responses. Let's break this down into manageable parts. Write using a dynamic tone and energetic writing style.

MINDSET

Operational - Efficiency - Barriers

Goal

To provide team leaders with a thorough framework for assessing the barriers or obstacles that prevent their team from acting on their priorities or ideas. This framework aims to uncover both internal and external factors hindering progress, allowing for tailored interventions to remove or mitigate these barriers and to help the team achieve their objectives effectively.

Prompt

Act as a **Business Strategy Consultant** specializing in **operational efficiency** for the **healthcare services industry**. Could you provide an **all-encompassing guide** on **the assessment of what is hindering my team from taking action on their current priorities or ideas**? I'm interested in **specific diagnostic tools such as questionnaires, SWOT analyses, and real-time feedback mechanisms**. Please segment the **guide** into **clear sections covering identification, analysis, and solution implementation**. Reveal lesser-known practices and innovative techniques. Let's systematically explore each facet. Write using a **visionary** tone and **innovative** writing style.

Formula

Act as a **[profession]** specializing in **[topic/expertise]** for the **[industry]**. Could you provide an **[all-encompassing guide/manual/resource]** on **[contextual challenge/opportunity]**? I'm interested in **[types of methods/approaches/tools]**. Please segment the **[guide/resource]** into **[stages/sections/steps]**. Reveal lesser-known practices and innovative techniques. Let's systematically explore each facet. Write using a **[type]** tone and **[style]** writing style.

Examples

Example 1: Act as an Organizational Psychologist with a focus on team dynamics for the asset management industry. Could you develop a comprehensive guide to identifying and overcoming barriers that prevent my team from focusing on their priorities? I am particularly interested in psychological assessments and observational techniques. Structure the guide into problem identification, psychological underpinnings, and actionable solutions, incorporating scholarly articles and empirical evidence. Highlight imaginative thoughts and avant-garde solutions. Let's piece-by-piece analyze this matter. Write using an academic tone and a scholarly writing style.

Example 2: Act as an Agile Coach specializing in team productivity. Could you supply an extensive guide on how to assess what prevents my team from acting on their key priorities? I'm focused on integrating agile methodologies and real-time tracking software into the diagnostic process. Break down the guide into the agile cycle stages of planning, diagnosing, acting, and reviewing. Include testimonials from other teams who successfully addressed similar issues. Present novel interpretations and visionary possibilities. Let's carefully evaluate each segment. Write using an agile mindset tone and an action-oriented writing style.

PROMPT No 60

Comfort - Productivity - Workplace

Goal

To understand the unique comfort preferences of each team member in order to create an inclusive and productive work environment. The focus will be on identifying the various factors, such as physical settings, work styles, communication preferences, and interpersonal dynamics, that contribute to each team member's comfort and productivity.

Prompt

Act as a **workplace culture consultant** with a specialization in **employee well-being** for the **IT sector**. Could you guide me through **the process of setting up work conditions where each of my team members feels most comfortable**? Please include **the steps for identifying individual comfort preferences and integrating them into a cohesive workplace strategy**. Make sure to cover how **these conditions will be communicated, measured, and periodically reviewed**. Probe into nonconformist solutions and divergent viewpoints to continually adapt and refine our approach. Let's dissect this in a structured manner. Write using a personable tone and an instructive writing style.

Formula

Act as a **[profession]** with a specialization in **[area of expertise]** for the **[industry]**. Could you guide me through **[specific challenge/opportunity]**? Please include **[methods/techniques]**. Make sure to cover how **[key areas/topics]**. Probe into nonconformist solutions and divergent viewpoints to continually adapt and refine our approach. Let's dissect this in a structured manner. Write using a **[type]** tone and **[style]** writing style.

Examples

Example 1: Act as an organizational psychologist with a specialization in interpersonal relationships for the hospitality industry. Can you help me identify the best practices to foster a comfortable and inclusive work environment, considering the diverse preferences of my team members? Include surveys and one-on-one interviews as methods. Make sure to discuss how these comfort-enhancing strategies will be communicated and reviewed. Navigate through unexplored realms and revolutionary paradigms to ensure a comfortable setting for all. Write using a considerate tone and an analytical writing style.

Example 2: Act as an HR advisor with a specialization in remote work strategies for the legal sector. Could you guide me on how to create a remote work environment where each team member feels comfortable and can be their most productive? Include steps for consultation and feedback. Make sure to cover the criteria to assess the effectiveness of these remote work conditions. Offer extraordinary advice and non-mainstream opinions to keep our remote work culture fresh and engaging. Write using an exploratory tone and a case-study writing style.

PROMPT No 61

Goal

To provide leaders with a comprehensive framework for initiating and managing sensitive conversations with their team members about potential dissatisfaction with their current roles or positions. The aim is to open channels of communication, collect honest feedback, and identify actionable solutions while maintaining a psychologically safe environment.

Prompt

Act as an **Executive Coach** specializing in **Employee Engagement and Retention** for the **food & beverage manufacturing industry.** Could you provide a **detailed guide** on how to **skillfully initiate and handle a delicate conversation with my team regarding where they'd rather be if they had a choice, compared to their current positions?** I am interested in **techniques that encourage openness, reduce defensiveness, and elicit actionable insights.** Include **questions, prompts, potential answers to expect, and guidance on interpreting and acting on the feedback** and organize the guide into **sections such as setting the stage, initiating the conversation, and following through with actionable steps.** Explore unconventional solutions and alternative perspectives. Let's sequentially address each element. Write using a **professional** tone and **clear** writing style.

Formula

Act as a **[profession]** specializing in **[topic/expertise]** for the **[industry]**. Could you provide a **[comprehensive guide/list/resource]** on how to **[specific challenge/opportunity]**? I am interested in **[focus areas/techniques]**. Include **[question/prompts/examples]** and organize the guide into **[sections/stages]**. Explore unconventional solutions and alternative perspectives. Let's sequentially address each element. Write using a **[type]** tone and **[style]** writing style.

Examples

Example 1: Act as a Communications Strategist specializing in Difficult Conversations. Could you furnish a complete roadmap on how to discuss potentially sensitive issues, like dissatisfaction with current roles, within my engineering team? I would like to focus on non-verbal communication techniques and cues that can assist in gauging true feelings without the team having to explicitly state them. Divide the roadmap into phases such as preparation, execution, and follow-up, providing key steps for each. Unearth hidden gems and non-traditional methods. Let's methodically dissect each component. Write using a visionary tone and innovative writing style.

Example 2: Act as a Human Resources Expert focusing on Employee Satisfaction. Could you produce a comprehensive toolkit to aid in discussing the uncomfortable topic of where my team members would rather be as opposed to their current roles? I am keen on understanding how to create a psychologically safe space for these conversations and how to use validated HR instruments for data collection. Segment the toolkit into areas like setting the groundwork, initiating dialogue, collecting data, and making improvements. Delve into uncharted territories and groundbreaking concepts. Let's scrutinize this topic incrementally. Write using an optimistic tone and positive writing style.

Tags

Alignment - Goal-Setting - Entertainment

Goal

To equip leaders with a comprehensive toolkit for engaging their teams in thoughtful discussions about what they seek to gain from specific experiences or challenges. The aim is to enhance clarity, alignment, and purpose, thereby enabling both individual and collective growth. This will involve creating a space for self-reflection, articulation of personal and team goals, and identifying pathways to achieve those goals.

Prompt

Act as an **Executive Coach** specializing in **Team Alignment and Goal-Setting** for the **entertainment industry**. Could you provide a **detailed guide** on how to **approach a conversation with my team regarding what they most want to gain from a specific experience or challenge**? I am interested in **methodologies that facilitate self-discovery and teamwork, including frameworks for goal-setting**. Include **question prompts, interactive exercises, and even digital tools that could assist in this process**. Organize the guide into **key components such as setting the stage, opening the discussion, diving deeper, and wrapping up with action plans**. Offer extraordinary advice and non-mainstream opinions. Let's think about this step by step. Write using a **dynamic** tone and **energetic** writing style.

Formula

Act as a **[profession]** specializing in **[topic/expertise]** for the **[industry]**. Could you provide a **[comprehensive guide/list/resource]** on how to **[specific challenge/opportunity]**? I am interested in **[focus areas/techniques]**. Include **[questions/prompts/examples]**. Organize the guide into **[sections/stages]**. Offer extraordinary advice and non-mainstream opinions. Let's think about this step by step. Write using a **[type]** tone and **[style]** writing style.

Examples

Example 1: Act as an Organizational Development Specialist focusing on Personal Development. Could you produce an exhaustive guide on facilitating conversations with my remote team about what they most want to gain from a team-building retreat? I am keen on using proven psychological models to guide this discussion. Please suggest a range of interactive exercises and reflective questions we can utilize before, during, and after the retreat. Divide the guide into segments such as preparation, real-time engagement, and post-retreat reflection. Reveal lesser-known practices and innovative techniques. Let's dissect this carefully. Write using a consultative tone and advisory writing style.

Example 2: Act as a Leadership Trainer specializing in Employee Engagement. Could you offer a structured guide on how to talk with my customer service team about what they most want to get from an upcoming customer interaction training? I'm looking for insights on the best ways to incorporate real-time feedback mechanisms and follow-up activities. Please include suggestions for both group activities and individual self-assessment tools. Arrange the guide into sections like pre-training considerations, training-day activities, and follow-up strategies. Highlight imaginative thoughts and avant-garde solutions. Let's break this down into manageable parts. Write using a responsive tone and customer-centric writing style.

PROMPT No 63

Tags

Resilience - Coping - Oil-and-Gas

Goal

To provide strategies and techniques for individuals and teams to endure and overcome challenging periods at work. These difficult times may include heightened stress, project failures, interpersonal conflicts, organizational changes, or other work-related challenges. The focus is on resilience, coping mechanisms, support systems, positive thinking, and actionable steps to navigate through these difficulties.

Prompt

Act as a **Resilience Coach** specializing in the Oil & Gas industry. During **challenging** periods at work, such as **meeting tight deadlines**, what are the **effective** strategies that **professionals** can **adopt**? How can **emotional intelligence** play a role in enduring these times? What **methodologies** can be **implemented** within a **team** to foster **resilience and adaptability**? Share **real-life examples** that **demonstrate** the **successful** application of these methodologies. Respond separately to each question. Explore unconventional solutions and alternative perspectives. Let's approach this methodically. Write using an **empathetic** tone and **constructive** writing style.

Formula

Act as a [profession] specializing in the [industry]. During [challenging/difficult/stressful] periods at work, such as [list specific situations], what are the [effective/practical/proven] strategies that [professionals/individuals/teams] can [adopt/implement/employ]? How can [list qualities or approaches like mindfulness, teamwork], play a role in [enduring/overcoming/navigating] these times? What [tools/methodologies/systems] can be [implemented/utilized/applied] within a [team/group/organization] to foster [resilience/adaptability/positivity]? Share [real-life/actual/practical] [examples/case studies/scenarios] that [demonstrate/illustrate/showcase] the [successful/effective/proven] application of these strategies. Respond separately to each question. Explore unconventional solutions and alternative perspectives. Let's approach this methodically. Write using a [type] tone and [style] writing style.

Examples

Example 1: Act as a Leadership Trainer specializing in the tech industry, during tough times such as project failures or tight deadlines, what are the proven strategies that teams can employ? How can open communication, flexibility, time management, and a focus on well-being play a role in overcoming these challenges? What training programs, workshops, or team-building activities can be utilized within a tech company to enhance resilience and adaptability? Share practical examples from successful tech companies that have navigated through similar situations. Respond separately to each question. Reveal lesser-known practices and innovative techniques. Let's arrange your response in a logical order. Write using a confident tone and analytical writing style.

Example 2: Act as a Team Development Specialist specializing in the healthcare industry, during stressful periods like handling medical emergencies or adapting to new regulations, what are the practical strategies that medical professionals can adopt? How can empathy, collaboration, continuous training, and a supportive work environment contribute to enduring these times? What mentoring programs, peer support, or crisis management plans can be implemented within a healthcare setting to ensure the well-being and effectiveness of the staff? Share real-life case studies from renowned healthcare institutions that have successfully dealt with such challenges. Respond separately to each question. Provide an exhaustive and all-encompassing analysis. Let's analyze this from multiple angles. Write using an inspirational tone and descriptive writing style.

OPTIONS

PROMPT No 64

Tags

Decision-Making - Development - Strategy

Goal

To empower team leaders, managers, and executives with a holistic strategy for fostering a growth mindset within their teams. By re-framing challenges as learning opportunities, you can boost team morale, enhance problem-solving skills, and contribute to ongoing professional development.

Prompt

Act as a **Leadership Coach** specializing in **growth mindset training** for the **manufacturing industry**. Could you guide me through a structured method to teach my team to approach problems as opportunities for learning? I want to understand how to **instill a growth mindset, encourage creative problem-solving, and promote collaborative learning**. Please provide a **best practices** that can be incorporated into our daily interactions and team meetings. Also, identify any potential obstacles and how we can mitigate them. Deliver a rigorous and thoroughgoing examination. Let's dissect this carefully. Write using an **enlightening** tone and an **analytical** writing style.

Formula

Act as a **[profession]** specializing in **[topic/specialization]** for the **[industry]**. Could you guide me through **[contextual challenge/opportunity]**? I want to understand **[desired objective]**. Please provide **[specific tools/best practices/actionable tips]** that can be integrated into our daily interactions and team meetings. Also, identify any potential obstacles and how we can mitigate them. Deliver a rigorous and thoroughgoing examination. Let's dissect this carefully. Write using a **[type]** tone and **[style]** writing style.

Examples

Example 1: Act as a Team Development Consultant specializing in resilience and adaptability for the finance industry. Could you provide me with a comprehensive guide to help my analysts see challenges as avenues for professional growth? I'm interested in enhancing their analytical skills and emotional intelligence. Offer specific exercises, discussion guidelines, and success metrics that we can use in our weekly team huddles. Also, point out any pitfalls like overconfidence and how we can avoid them. Create a systematic and far-reaching overview. Let's explore this step-by-step. Write using a methodical tone and a systematic writing style.

Example 2: Act as a Corporate Training Specialist specializing in critical thinking and innovation for the tech sector. Can you show me how to get my development team to view technical glitches as chances for improvement and innovation? I'd like to focus on fostering a culture of continuous learning and improvement. Suggest coding kata exercises, hackathons, and relevant KPIs for monitoring success. Also, identify challenges like cognitive biases that could hinder progress and how we can address them. Render an in-depth and wide-spectrum exploration. Let's break this down point by point. Write using an insightful tone and a strategic writing style.

PROMPT No 65

Tags
Risk-Mitigation - Opportunity-Leverage - Analysis

Goal
To equip your team with the ability to discern the critical factors, both internal and external, that could significantly influence their projects or daily work. This includes understanding methodologies, tools, and strategic thinking to analyze the environment, stakeholders, risks, and opportunities, leading to informed decisions and successful outcomes.

Prompt
Act as a **Project Management Expert** specializing in the **software development industry**. Could you guide me on how my team can **systematically identify the factors that may have the most substantial impact on their projects or work**? We are looking to **both mitigate risks and leverage opportunities, considering various aspects like market trends, stakeholder expectations, technological advancements, regulations, and internal dynamics**. Please provide a comprehensive response, including applicable frameworks, analytical tools, and best practices. Let's analyze this piece by piece. Write using an **informative** tone and **analytical** writing style.

Formula
Act as a **[profession]** specializing in the **[industry]**. Could you guide me on how my team can **[contextual challenge/opportunity]**? We are looking to **[desired outcome]**, considering various aspects like **[specific factors or conditions]**. Please provide a comprehensive response, including applicable frameworks, analytical tools, and best practices. Let's analyze this piece by piece. Write using a **[type]** tone and **[style]** writing style.

Examples

Example 1: Act as a Risk Management Specialist specializing in the construction industry. Could you instruct me on how my team can discern the elements that could profoundly affect our construction projects? We are aiming to navigate uncertainties and capitalize on favorable circumstances, examining aspects like regulatory compliance, environmental conditions, stakeholder relationships, safety protocols, and material supply. Please share insights into risk assessment matrices, scenario planning, and collaboration techniques. Let's dissect this carefully. Write using a professional tone and methodical writing style.

Example 2: Act as a Strategic Planning Consultant specializing in the retail sector. Could you advise me on how my team can pinpoint the factors that may dramatically influence our retail operations or initiatives? We are focused on minimizing setbacks and harnessing potential gains, looking at aspects such as consumer behavior, competitive landscape, technological innovation, supply chain efficiency, and market regulations. Please outline detailed approaches including SWOT analysis, Porter's Five Forces, trend analysis, and agile methodologies. Let's take this one step at a time. Write using a confident tone and strategic writing style.

PROMPT No 66

Tags
Leadership   Improvement Finance

Goal
To equip team leaders, managers, and executives with a robust methodology for effectively conversing with their team members about areas they wish to improve. By doing this, leadership can cultivate an environment of continuous growth and skill development, thereby boosting job satisfaction and performance.

Prompt
Act as a **Professional Development Strategist** specializing in **individual growth and performance** for the **finance industry**. Could you guide me through **a detailed framework to effectively discuss areas of improvement with my team?** The goal is to **establish a culture of continuous growth and professional development**. Your approach should offer a step-by-step conversation guide, key questions, and follow-up mechanisms, all designed to inspire honesty and actionable insights. Let's dissect this topic methodically. Write using an **encouraging** tone and an **analytical** writing style.

Formula
Act as a **[profession]** specializing in **[topic/specialization]** for the **[industry]**. Could you guide me through **[contextual challenge/opportunity]**? The objective is to **[desired outcome]**. Your response should be comprehensive, covering all relevant aspects and displaying an exceptional level of precision and quality. Let's dissect this topic methodically. Write using a **[type]** tone and **[style]** writing style.

Examples

Example 1: Act as a Team Development Coach specializing in the tech industry. Could you provide me with a comprehensive guide to effectively discuss professional growth opportunities with my engineering team? The objective is to enable them to identify areas in which they want to excel and thereby align those with the team's skill-building initiatives. Your advice should include relevant talking points, sensitive yet probing questions, and a framework for conducting follow-up sessions to track progress. Let's go over this in detail. Write using a supportive tone and a focused writing style.

Example 2: Act as a Leadership Mentor specializing in the healthcare industry. Could you walk me through an actionable process for holding discussions about career development with my nursing staff? The aim is to engage them in open conversations about areas they feel need improvement or expansion. Your recommendations should encompass an outline for structured conversations, a list of questions that encourage introspection and openness, and a method for synthesizing this information into actionable growth plans. Let's examine every aspect carefully. Write using an empathetic tone and a thorough writing style.

PERFORMANCE

PROMPT No 67

Tags

Outcomes - Alignment - Clarity

Goal

To provide leaders with a step-by-step guide on how to initiate and carry out a meaningful discussion with their teams about defining the ideal outcomes of their work. The conversation is designed to encourage clarity, mutual understanding, and alignment with broader company objectives, thereby leading to enhanced job satisfaction and productivity.

Prompt

As an **Executive Coach** with a specialization in **outcome-based team management** for the **healthcare sector**, could you guide me through **the process of conducting a conversation with my team to articulate what they consider the ideal outcome of their work to be?** Please include **tactics for initiating the conversation, specific questions that encourage vision setting, and strategies for harmonizing individual visions with organizational goals.** Ensure the guide covers **how to elicit both tangible and intangible outcomes, as well as ways to track and measure these outcomes for future assessment.** Introduce novel approaches and emerging paradigms. Let's examine this in a structured manner. Write using an **authoritative** tone and **factual** writing style.

Formula

As a **[profession]** with specialization in **[focus area]** for the **[industry]**, could you guide me through **[contextual challenge/opportunity]**? Please include **[methods/techniques]**. Ensure the guide covers **[aspects/topics to be addressed]**. Introduce novel approaches and emerging paradigms. Let's examine this in a structured manner. Write using a **[type]** tone and **[style]** writing style.

Examples

Example 1: As a Leadership Development Expert specializing in project management in the finance industry, could you walk me through the steps to discuss with my team the ideal outcomes they aim to achieve in our upcoming projects? Include icebreakers to start the conversation, probing questions for aligning individual aspirations with team goals, and methods for setting measurable outcomes. Ensure the guide delves into setting KPIs and aligning them with corporate strategy. Reveal future-focused strategies like predictive analytics. Let's unpack this layer by layer. Write using an instructive tone and an analytical writing style.

Example 2: As a Team Dynamics Consultant with a focus on remote teams in the tech sector, could you help me outline a strategy for facilitating a conversation with my distributed team about their ideal work outcomes? Include approaches to engage remote team members, questions to explore both qualitative and quantitative goals, and steps for integrating these individual goals into a cohesive team vision. Make sure the guide touches upon leveraging tech tools for tracking and measurement. Introduce digital trends and virtual engagement methods. Let's delineate this logically. Write using a consultative tone and a systematic writing style.

PROMPT No 68

Goals - Prioritization - Repercussions

To assist leaders in identifying critical company goals that, if overlooked or not pursued, could have significant negative repercussions for the business. This includes evaluating the long-term vision, operational necessities, and the economic, social, and environmental impact of not pursuing certain goals.

Act as a **business strategist** with a specialization i **enterprise risk management** for the **healthcare industry.** Could you guide me through **the methodology for identifying the goal that, if not pursued, would have the most substantial negative impact on my organization?** Please include a **SWOT analysis, prioritization matrix, and stakeholder input.** Make sure to cover how **this identified critical goal aligns with or deviates from the overall company strategy.** Navigate through unexplored realms and revolutionary paradigms to determine the business risk. Let's dissect this in a structured manner. Write using a **pragmatic** tone and a **scholarly** writing style.

Act as a [profession] with a specialization in [area of expertise] for the [industry]. Could you guide me through [specific challenge/opportunity]? Please include [methods/techniques]. Make sure to cover how [key areas/topics]. [Navigate through unexplored realms and revolutionary paradigms to determine the business risk. Let's dissect this in a structured manner. Write using a [type] tone and [style] writing style.

Example 1: Act as a financial analyst with a specialization in economic impact assessment for the e-commerce sector. Could you guide me through a process to identify which unaddressed business goal could severely affect our financial stability? Please include cost-benefit analysis, risk profiles, and market research. Make sure to cover the financial aspects and how this unaddressed goal could impact shareholder value. Conduct an intensive and all-inclusive study to navigate through financial intricacies. Write using a data-driven tone and an investigative writing style.

Example 2: Act as a sustainability expert with a specialization in corporate responsibility for the automotive industry. Can you help me identify the sustainability goal that, if neglected, could significantly tarnish our brand reputation? Include stakeholder mapping, environmental audits, and social impact assessments. Make sure to explain how this neglected goal could affect our public relations and compliance with regulations. Delve into uncharted territories and groundbreaking concepts to understand reputational risk. Write using a cautionary tone and an expositional writing style.

PROMPT No 69

Tags

Leadership - Collaboration - OrganizationalCulture

Goal

To assist team leaders, managers, or individuals within a corporate context to identify and instill values that can guide a team toward realizing their potential, fostering collaboration, enhancing performance, and aligning with organizational goals. The ultimate aim is to provide actionable insights that can be customized to various team dynamics and organizational structures.

Prompt

Act as an **Organizational Culture Consultant** specializing in **value-driven team development** for the **broadcasting industry**. Could you delineate the **core values that could direct my team toward realizing their fullest potential**? This includes insights into **how these values can be embedded into daily practices, and how they can align with various organizational goals and industry norms**. Provide applicable examples, strategies, and overlooked opportunities, considering different team dynamics, organizational structures, and the **broadcasting industry**. Let's dissect this systematically. Write using an **analytical** tone and a **strategic** writing style.

Formula

Act as a **[profession]** specializing in **[specific focus]** for the **[industry]**. Could you delineate the **[contextual challenge/opportunity]**? This includes insights into **[specific requirements]**. Provide applicable examples, strategies, and overlooked opportunities, considering different team dynamics, organizational structures, and the **[industry]**. Let's dissect this systematically. Write using a **[type]** tone and **[style]** writing style.

Examples

Example 1: Act as a Leadership Coach specializing in the technology industry. Could you detail the fundamental values that a tech team could adopt to foster innovation, collaboration, and growth?

This includes insights into how these values can be reflected in project management, team interactions, and alignment with company vision. Provide unique strategies, success stories, and potential pitfalls, considering various team sizes, organizational hierarchies, and technological domains. Let's analyze this meticulously. Write using a focused tone and a thoughtful writing style.

Example 2: Act as a Corporate Culture Strategist specializing in small businesses and startups. Could you outline the key values that a fledgling team could cultivate to build a robust culture, enhance productivity, and drive success? This includes insights into how these values can be integrated into recruitment, training, and daily operations, and align with the unique needs of small businesses. Provide hands-on recommendations, innovative approaches, and industry benchmarks, considering various sectors, growth stages, and entrepreneurial challenges. Let's explore this comprehensively. Write using an engaging tone and a practical writing style.

PREFERENCES

PROMPT No 70

Tags
Prioritization - Facilitation - Reflection

Goal
To equip team leaders with the necessary skills and approaches to guide their teams through a thoughtful reflection process. The focus is on what actions or decisions they would prioritize if they knew they had limited time. This exercise aims to clarify priorities, streamline focus, and inspire meaningful action.

Prompt
Act as a **Life Prioritization Coach** specializing in the **financial services industry**. Could you outline **a structured approach to help me prepare my team to reflect on what actions or decisions they would prioritize if they knew they had limited time left**? This should encompass **guided reflective exercises, pointed questions, and tips for facilitating an open and safe discussion**. This is crucial for **enhancing team focus, commitment, and overall productivity**. Uncover scarce wisdom and trailblazing ideas. Let's dissect each facet of this approach. Write using a **motivational** tone and a **detailed, step-by-step** writing style.

Formula
Act as a **[profession]** specializing in **[industry]**. Could you outline **[contextual challenge/opportunity]**? This should encompass **[approaches/techniques/tools]**. This is crucial for **[desired outcomes]**. Uncover scarce wisdom and trailblazing ideas. Let's dissect each facet of this approach. Write using a **[type]** tone and **[style]** writing style.

Examples

Example 1: Act as an Organizational Psychologist specializing in the manufacturing sector. Could you provide a comprehensive strategy for preparing my factory team to contemplate the actions or decisions they would take if they knew their time on a project was limited? Include activities that prompt self-reflection, questions that provoke thought, and methods for encouraging a candid discussion. Furnish exceptional counsel and offbeat perspectives. This is vital for project effectiveness and individual growth. Let's break down each element. Write using an empathetic tone and a research-based writing style.

Example 2: Act as a Leadership Development Coach specializing in the nonprofit sector. Could you delineate an approach to help my team of volunteers reflect on their priorities, assuming they had only a short time to make an impact? The framework should cover self-reflection activities, deep-dive questions, and techniques to foster an open dialogue. This is important for maximizing our mission-driven focus and improving overall team morale. Disclose underutilized practices and state-of-the-art wisdom. Let's explore each component. Write using an inspiring tone and an action-oriented writing style.

PRIORITIES

PROMPT No 71

Tags

PositiveCulture - Communication - Team-building

Goal

To equip leaders, managers, and executives with an in-depth framework to cultivate and sustain a positive work culture within their organizations. Implementing this framework will lead to higher employee morale, better team collaboration, and ultimately, enhanced organizational performance.

Prompt

Act as an **Organizational Culture Specialist** specializing in the **cultivation of positive work environments** for the **automotive industry**. Could you provide a **multi-faceted plan to instill a culture of positivity within my organization**? Your plan should address **leadership behaviors, team-building activities, communication strategies, and metrics for evaluating the success of these initiatives**. Impart an all-encompassing and rigorous plan. Let's break down each component for better understanding. Write using a **strategic** tone and a **solution-oriented** writing style.

Formula

Act as a **[profession]** specializing in **[topic/specialization]** for the **[industry]**. Could you provide **[contextual challenge/opportunity]**? The plan should address **[desired outcomes and considerations]**. Impart an all-encompassing and rigorous plan. Let's break down each component for better understanding. Write using a **[type]** tone and **[style]** writing style.

Examples

Example 1: Act as a Leadership Development Coach specializing in the technology sector. Could you offer a comprehensive strategy to build a positive work culture in my fast-paced software development firm? The plan should cover leadership's role in modeling positive behaviors, the types of team-building exercises that can foster a positive environment, effective modes of communication, and key performance indicators to gauge the effectiveness of these efforts. Highlight imaginative thoughts and avant-garde solutions. Let's scrutinize each part in detail. Write using an analytical tone and a meticulous writing style.

Example 2: Act as a Corporate Well-being Consultant specializing in the healthcare industry. Could you guide me through a detailed framework for fostering a culture of positivity in a hospital setting, where stress and burnout are common? Your framework should outline how senior medical staff can exhibit positivity, activities that can bring the medical team together, communication channels that need to be optimized, and metrics to assess the program's success. Present novel interpretations and visionary possibilities. Let's explore each facet thoroughly. Write using an empathetic tone and an evidence-based writing style.

PROGRESS

PROMPT No 72

Learning - Development - Professionalism

To equip team leaders and managers with the insight and understanding to identify key indicators, milestones, or signposts within the learning process of their team members. This knowledge will help in recognizing progress, diagnosing challenges, and facilitating personalized support, thereby leading to more efficient learning and professional development within the team.

Act as a **Learning and Development Specialist** specializing in the **e-commerce industry**. Could you elucidate the **essential signposts or milestones that my team can recognize in their learning process**? This includes **identifying when they are grasping new concepts, struggling with particular subjects, reaching a plateau, or excelling in certain areas**. Recognizing these signposts is critical for **adapting our training programs, providing timely assistance, and celebrating achievements**. Please deliver an exhaustive guide that details various methods, best practices, and tools to **observe these indicators, both individually and collectively**. Let's explore this systematically. Write using an **informative** tone and **engaging** writing style.

Act as a **[profession]** specializing in the **[industry]**. Could you elucidate the **[contextual challenge/opportunity]**? This includes **[specific factors or elements]**. Recognizing these signposts is critical for **[desired outcome]**. Please deliver an exhaustive guide that details various methods, best practices, and tools to **[action or approach]**. Let's explore this systematically. Write using a **[type]** tone and **[style]** writing style.

Example 1: Act as a Professional Development Coach specializing in the finance industry. Could you help me identify the key indicators or signposts that my finance team can observe in their professional development process? This encompasses understanding new financial tools, mastering risk analysis, or requiring further guidance in compliance issues. Detecting these milestones is essential for personalizing support, enhancing capabilities, and ensuring alignment with industry standards. Please provide a comprehensive method, incorporating self-assessment tools, peer reviews, manager evaluations, and ongoing feedback loops. Let's approach this analytically. Write using a professional tone and analytical writing style.

Example 2: Act as an Educational Technology Expert specializing in the non-profit sector. Could you guide me through the distinct landmarks or signs that my team members can watch for in their technological skill-building journey? This involves the realization of new digital tools, challenges with specific software, or excellence in data management. Pinpointing these markers is vital for aligning training resources, fostering a culture of continuous learning, and connecting technological skills with organizational mission. Please craft a nuanced and practical guide, weaving in online assessment platforms, mentorship programs, self-directed learning paths, and collaborative learning spaces. Let's examine this with creativity. Write using an inspirational tone and constructive writing style.

PROMPT No 73

Performance - Measurement - Team

To understand various comprehensive measures and systems that can be implemented to track the progress or performance of a team, with an emphasis on all-encompassing solutions that fit various organizational contexts.

Act as a **Performance Coach** specializing in the **recruitment industry**. Could you delineate **the various measures or systems that I can implement to meticulously track the progress or performance of my team?** This is pivotal for **ensuring alignment with goals, identifying areas for improvement, and fostering a culture of continuous growth within the team.** Please provide an all-encompassing and comprehensive explanation with detailed actions to follow, covering different methodologies, tools, software, and best practices. Let's take this one step at a time. Write using a **confident** tone and **analytical** writing style.

Act as a **[profession]** specializing in the **[industry]**. Could you delineate **[contextual challenge/opportunity]**? This is pivotal for **[desired outcome]**. Please provide an all-encompassing and comprehensive explanation with detailed actions to follow, covering different methodologies, tools, software, and best practices. Let's take this one step at a time. Write using a **[type]** tone and **[style]** writing style.

Example 1: Act as a Team Building Specialist specializing in the healthcare industry. Could you delineate the specific methods and tools to track teamwork and collaboration within a medical team? Provide unique insights and overlooked opportunities. Let's dissect this carefully. Write using an instructive tone and engaging writing style.

Example 2: Act as an Employee Performance Specialist specializing in the manufacturing industry. Could you delineate the systems to monitor and evaluate the performance of assembly line workers? Propose a comprehensive and elaborate depiction, considering both manual and automated approaches. Let's analyze this piece by piece. Write using a professional tone and persuasive writing style.

PURPOSE

PROMPT No 74

Tags
Self-awareness - Career Trajectory - Introspection

Goal
To aid in identifying recurring themes, patterns, or common threads in one's professional career, enabling deeper self-awareness and alignment with personal values and goals.

Prompt
Act as a **Career Development Coach** specializing in the **information technology industry**. Could you guide me through the process of identifying **the recurring theme or common thread that has been present throughout my professional career**? The ultimate goal is to **gain a profound understanding of my career trajectory, recognizing underlying patterns that can guide my future career decisions**. Share distinctive guidance, tools for introspection, and methods to connect my past and present roles, considering various career stages and transitions. Let's analyze this step by step. Write using an **insightful** tone and **reflective** writing style.

Formula
Act as a **[profession]** specializing in the **[industry]**. Could you guide me through the process of identifying **[contextual challenge/opportunity]**? The ultimate goal is to **[explicit desired outcome]**. Share distinctive guidance, tools for introspection, and methods to connect my past and present roles, considering various career stages and transitions. Let's analyze this step by step. Write using a **[type]** tone and **[style]** writing style.

Examples

Example 1: Act as a Personal Growth Consultant specializing in the education industry. Could you guide me through the process of finding the recurring theme in my teaching career? The ultimate goal is to align my teaching methods and subjects with my core values and passions. Share guidance, reflective exercises, and actionable steps, considering different educational settings and phases of my career. Let's take this one step at a time. Write using an empathetic tone and thoughtful writing style.

Example 2: Act as a Professional Development Specialist specializing in the automotive industry. Could you guide me through the process of identifying the common thread in my engineering career? The ultimate goal is to align my skills, projects, and contributions with industry needs and personal interests. Share insights, diagnostic tools, and strategic planning methods, considering various technological trends and industry shifts. Let's dissect this carefully. Write using an analytical tone and precise writing style.

PROMPT No 75

Tags

Framework - Articulation - Collaboration

Goal

To obtain a comprehensive, actionable framework that outlines methods for defining and articulating in simple but engaging terms what one aims to achieve in collaboration with their team. The objective is to enhance team alignment, improve communication, and foster a collaborative work environment.

Prompt

As a **Communication Expert** in the **retail industry**, could you provide a **detailed toolkit** outlining **methods** to define in simple but engaging terms what **I** aim to achieve in collaboration with **my** team? Additionally, offer **actionable steps** for **immediate** implementation. Break down your insights into distinct modules, each supported by **evidence from reputable industry reports**. Investigate unexpected avenues and creative pathways. Let's **examine each dimension meticulously**. Write using a **captivating** tone and a **relatable** writing style.

Formula

As a [profession] in the [industry], could you provide a [comprehensive strategy/thorough toolkit/detailed blueprint] detailing [methods/techniques/approaches] to define in simple but engaging terms what [I/we/they] aim to achieve in collaboration with [my/our/their] team? Additionally, offer [actionable steps/initial measures/immediate tactics] for [immediate/short-term/long-term] implementation. Break down your insights into distinct modules, each supported by [evidence from/references from/data from] [reputable journals/credible research/authoritative publications/industry reports]. Investigate unexpected avenues and creative pathways. Let's [examine each dimension meticulously/dissect this carefully]. Write using a [captivating/inspiring/motivating] tone and a [relatable/engaging/innovative] writing style.

Examples

Example 1: As a Team Building Coach in the automotive sector, could you provide a comprehensive strategy outlining the techniques to define in simple but engaging terms what I aim to achieve in collaboration with my engineering team? Additionally, offer initial measures for short-term implementation. Break down your insights into distinct modules, each authenticated by corroborative evidence from credible sources. Explore unconventional approaches and diverse viewpoints. Let's dissect this carefully. Write using an inspiring tone and an engaging writing style.

Example 2: As a Leadership Development Consultant in the education sector, could you provide a thorough toolkit outlining the approaches I can employ to define in simple but engaging terms what I aim to achieve in collaboration with my faculty? Additionally, offer immediate tactics for long-term implementation. Break down your insights into distinct modules, each endorsed with data from verified academic publications. Unearth hidden gems and non-traditional methods. Let's examine each dimension meticulously. Write using a captivating tone and a relatable writing style.

PROMPT No 76

Tags
Decision-Making - Communication - Articulation

Goal
To provide team leaders and managers with actionable strategies and a structured framework to facilitate open conversations with their team members, allowing them to better articulate their needs, wants, and aspirations. This, in turn, will contribute to better decision-making, increased employee satisfaction, and a more cohesive work environment.

Prompt
Act as an **Executive Leadership Coach** specializing in **effective communication and decision-making** for the **financial industry**. Could you guide me through a **comprehensive method to help my team articulate what they really want when they are unsure themselves**? The method should incorporate **active listening techniques, questioning strategies, and frameworks for self-reflection and clarity**. Suggest fresh approaches and inventive strategies. Let's explore each component to ensure a well-rounded approach. Write using a **pragmatic** tone and a **precise** writing style.

Formula
Act as a [profession] specializing in [topic/specialization] for the [industry]. Could you guide me through [contextual challenge/opportunity]? The method should incorporate [desired outcomes/considerations]. Suggest fresh approaches and inventive strategies. Let's explore each component to ensure a well-rounded approach. Write using a [type] tone and [style] writing style.

Examples

Example 1: Act as a Team Development Consultant specializing in the technology sector. Could you walk me through a structured process to help my software engineers better define what they're looking for in their career paths, especially when they're uncertain? The approach should include various active listening exercises, probing question techniques, and tools for self-reflection that will help them gain more clarity. Produce a sweeping and meticulous response. Let's dissect each element of the approach carefully. Write using an engaging tone and an analytical writing style.

Example 2: Act as a Career Mentor specializing in the education sector. Could you assist me in establishing a system that helps my teaching staff articulate their pedagogical goals when they are unclear? Your plan should detail active listening mechanisms, appropriate questions to spur deeper thought, and reflective frameworks that enable more precise goal-setting. Extend a detailed and exhaustive response. Let's dive deep into each facet of the system. Write using a thoughtful tone and an instructive writing style.

PROMPT No 77

Self-Awareness - Media - Purpose

To acquire a comprehensive, actionable guide on methods for assessing where one currently stands in living in alignment with their purpose, with the aim of fostering self-awareness, personal growth, and professional alignment.

As a **Purpose-Alignment Coach** in the **media industry**, could you provide an exhaustive guide outlining the methods **I** can employ to assess where **I** currently am in living in alignment with **my purpose**? Please include **self-assessment tools**. Break down your advice into specific sections, reinforcing each with **quantifiable metrics and scholarly literature**. Explore unconventional approaches and diverse viewpoints. Let's dissect this carefully. Write using an **empathetic** tone and a **narrative** writing style.

As a **[profession]** in the **[industry]**, could you provide an exhaustive guide outlining the methods **[I/Name/Role]** can employ to assess where **[I/they]** currently am/are in living in alignment with **[my/their]** **[purpose/goals/values]**? Please include both **[self-assessment tools/reflective exercises]**. Break down your advice into specific sections, reinforcing each with **[quantifiable metrics/scholarly literature]**. Explore unconventional approaches and diverse viewpoints. Let's dissect this carefully. Write using a **[type]** tone and **[style]** writing style.

Example 1: As a Life Coach in the healthcare sector, could you provide an exhaustive guide outlining the methods a medical professional can employ to assess where they currently are in living in alignment with their caregiving purpose? Please include both psychometric tests and journaling exercises. Divide your insights into separate modules, each validated by empirical findings and authoritative sources. Investigate unexpected avenues and creative pathways. Let's examine each dimension meticulously. Write using a focused tone and a concise writing style.

Example 2: As a Career Development Specialist in the finance industry, could you provide an exhaustive guide outlining the methods I can employ to assess where I currently am in living in alignment with my professional goals? Please include both 360-degree feedback methods and mindfulness practices. Structure your guidance into individual components, each backed by statistical analysis and peer-reviewed studies. Unearth hidden gems and non-traditional methods. Let's tackle this in a phased manner. Write using a balanced tone and a nuanced writing style.

RELATIONSHIPS

PROMPT No 78

Tags

Roles - Construction - Allocation

Goal

To acquire a comprehensive, actionable framework for determining the responsibilities of team members for a specific project, with the aim of optimizing resource allocation, enhancing team collaboration, and ensuring project success.

Prompt

As a **Project Management Consultant** in the **construction industry**, could you provide a **detailed blueprint** outlining the **strategies I** can employ to determine the responsibilities of **my team members** for an **upcoming project**? Please include **both role-mapping exercises and communication protocols**. Divide your insights into separate modules, each **authenticated by corroborative evidence from credible sources**. Explore unconventional approaches and diverse viewpoints. Let's examine each dimension meticulously. Write using a consultative tone and a narrative writing style.

Formula

As a [profession] in the [industry], could you provide a [detailed blueprint/thorough toolkit/in-depth manual] outlining the [methods/tactics/strategies] [I/Name/Role] can employ to determine the responsibilities of [my/our/their] [team/group/department] for [a/an/the] [upcoming/current/specific] project? Please include both [role-mapping exercises/communication protocols/task delegation frameworks]. Divide your insights into separate modules, each [authenticated by/endorsed with] [corroborative evidence from/ data from/references from] [credible/reputable/authoritative] sources. Explore unconventional approaches and diverse viewpoints. Let's examine each dimension meticulously. Write using a [consultative/empathetic/balanced] tone and a [narrative/nuanced/concise] writing style.

Examples

Example 1: As a Team Dynamics Specialist in the technology sector, could you provide an in-depth manual outlining the methods a project manager can employ to determine the responsibilities of their software development team for an upcoming software release? Please include both role-definition templates and stakeholder communication plans. Structure your guidance into individual components, each endorsed with data from verified academic publications. Investigate unexpected avenues and creative pathways. Let's tackle this in a phased manner. Write using a focused tone and a nuanced writing style.

Example 2: As an Organizational Development Consultant in the retail industry, could you provide a thorough toolkit outlining the tactics I can employ to determine the responsibilities of my customer service team for the upcoming holiday season? Please include both task allocation algorithms and team briefing protocols. Break down your advice into specific sections, each supported with citations from reliable industry reports. Unearth hidden gems and non-traditional methods. Let's dissect this carefully. Write using an empathetic tone and a concise writing style.

PROMPT No 79

Tags

Relationships - Communication - Collaboration

Goal

To establish principles, techniques, and best practices for building supportive and trusting relationships with colleagues. This includes understanding the foundations of trust, effective communication, empathy, collaboration, and ongoing support within professional relationships.

Prompt

Act as a **Corporate Relationship Building and Leadership Coaching expert** specializing in the **food & beverage manufacturing industry**. Trust and support among colleagues are vital for a harmonious and productive working environment. How can a **professional** at any level **cultivate supportive and trusting** relationships with **colleagues**? What are some **principles** and **behaviors** that can be **adopted**? Provide a **comprehensive** guide that includes **understanding** the **nuances** of trust, **developing empathy**, **active listening**, **conflict resolution**, **collaboration**, and **ongoing support**. Include scenarios that **exemplify** how these principles can be **applied** in the **food & beverage manufacturing industry**.

Formula

Act as a **[profession]** specializing in the **[industry]**. Trust and support among colleagues are vital for a harmonious and productive working environment. How can a **[professional/individual/team member]** **[cultivate/build/develop]** **[supportive/trusting/positive]** relationships with **[colleagues/peers/team members]**? What are some **[principles/techniques/best practices]**, and **[behaviors/attitudes/strategies]** that can be **[adopted/implemented/fostered]**? Provide a **[comprehensive/thorough/complete]** guide that includes **[understanding/recognizing/identifying]** the **[nuances/elements/aspects]** of trust, **[developing/fostering/building]** **[empathy/compassion]**, **[active listening/effective communication]**, **[conflict resolution/problem-solving]**, **[collaboration/teamwork]**, and **[ongoing support/recognition/reinforcement]**. Include

[scenarios/case studies/examples] that **[exemplify/illustrate/demonstrate]** how these principles can be **[applied/utilized/enacted]** in the **[industry]**.

Example 1: Act as an Organizational Development Specialist in the manufacturing industry, where trust and collaboration are key to safety and efficiency. How can a floor supervisor cultivate supportive and trusting relationships with line workers? What principles such as transparency, open communication, mutual respect, clear expectations, and regular feedback can be applied? Provide a detailed guide with scenarios demonstrating how these principles can be effectively used in a manufacturing setting to enhance teamwork and productivity.

Example 2: Act as a Team Relationship Coach in a multinational corporation, where diversity and cultural nuances play a significant role in building trust. How can a project manager develop trusting relationships with team members across different regions and cultures? What techniques such as cultural awareness, empathy, inclusive communication, conflict management, and ongoing collaboration can be adopted? Provide comprehensive examples and case studies that illustrate how these strategies can be tailored to fit diverse teams within a global context, fostering a cohesive and trusting working environment.

PROMPT No 80

Presence - Engagement - Communication

To identify actionable strategies and techniques that can help an individual enhance the nature or quality of their presence in order to be fully engaged and present in various settings. This includes both professional and personal interactions, aiming to improve communication, leadership skills, and overall well-being.

As a **Mindfulness Expert** in the **healthcare industry**, could you provide a **detailed roadmap** for enhancing the **quality** of **my** presence to be **fully engaged and present** in **my** interactions? Include **actionable steps** for **long-term application**. Organize your insights into **thematic clusters**, each substantiated by **evidence from reputable journals**. Probe into **alternative perspectives and groundbreaking concepts**. Let's **deconstruct this subject stepwise**. Write using a **visionary** tone and an **invigorating** writing style.

As a **[profession]** in the **[industry]**, could you provide a **[detailed roadmap/comprehensive guide/structured plan]** for enhancing the **[quality/nature]** of **[my/our/their]** presence to be **[fully engaged/fully present/both]** in **[my/our/their]** interactions? Include **[actionable steps/practical solutions/immediate measures]** for **[immediate/short-term/long-term]** application. Organize your insights into **[thematic clusters/distinct categories/individual segments]**, each substantiated by **[evidence from/references from/data from]** **[reputable journals/credible research/authoritative** publications]. Probe into [alternative perspectives/groundbreaking concepts/innovative methods]. Let's [deconstruct this subject stepwise/examine each dimension meticulously]. Write using a [visionary/inspiring/empowering] tone and an [invigorating/energetic/engaging] writing style.

Example 1: As a Leadership Coach in the technology sector, could you provide a structured plan for enhancing the quality of my presence to be fully engaged in my interactions with my engineering team? Include practical solutions for immediate application. Organize your insights into distinct categories, each substantiated by references from credible research. Explore alternative perspectives and innovative methods. Let's examine each dimension meticulously. Write using an inspiring tone and an energetic writing style.

Example 2: As a Personal Development Consultant in the education sector, could you provide a comprehensive guide for enhancing the nature of my presence to be fully present in my interactions with students? Include immediate measures for long-term application. Organize your insights into individual segments, each substantiated by data from authoritative publications. Probe into groundbreaking concepts and innovative methods. Let's deconstruct this subject stepwise. Write using an empowering tone and an engaging writing style.

PROMPT No 81

Engagement - Persuasive - Organization

To obtain a comprehensive, actionable framework that outlines methods for creating a growth-mindset environment within a company and strategies for effectively communicating the benefits of such an environment to employees. The aim is to enhance employee engagement, improve performance, and contribute to overall organizational success.

As an **Organizational Psychologist** in the **technology sector**, could you provide a **detailed action plan** outlining **methods** to create a growth-mindset environment within **my** company and strategies to effectively communicate its benefits to employees? Additionally, offer **actionable steps** for **mid-term** implementation. Divide your insights into distinct modules, each supported by **evidence from reputable industry reports**. Investigate unexpected avenues and creative pathways. Let's **examine each dimension meticulously**. Write using a **persuasive** tone and a **visionary** writing style.

As a [profession] in the [industry], could you provide a [comprehensive strategy/thorough toolkit/detailed action plan] outlining [methods/techniques/approaches] to create a growth-mindset environment within [my/our/their] company and strategies to effectively communicate its benefits to employees? Additionally, offer [actionable steps/initial measures/immediate tactics] for [short-term/mid-term/long-term] implementation. Divide your insights into distinct modules, each supported by [evidence from/references from/data from] [reputable journals/credible research/authoritative publications/industry reports]. Investigate unexpected avenues and creative pathways. Let's [examine each dimension meticulously/dissect this carefully]. Write using a [persuasive/inspiring/motivating] tone and a [visionary/engaging/innovative] writing style.

Example 1: As a Human Resources Consultant in the healthcare sector, could you provide a comprehensive strategy outlining the techniques to create a growth-mindset environment within my hospital and strategies to effectively communicate its benefits to medical staff? Additionally, offer initial measures for short-term implementation. Divide your insights into distinct modules, each authenticated by corroborative evidence from credible sources. Explore unconventional approaches and diverse viewpoints. Let's dissect this carefully. Write using an inspiring tone and an engaging writing style.

Example 2: As a Leadership Development Coach in the finance industry, could you provide a thorough toolkit outlining the approaches I can employ to create a growth-mindset environment within my investment firm and strategies to effectively communicate its benefits to analysts and managers? Additionally, offer immediate tactics for long-term implementation. Divide your insights into distinct modules, each endorsed with data from verified academic publications. Unearth hidden gems and non-traditional methods. Let's examine each dimension meticulously. Write using a persuasive tone and an innovative writing style.

PROMPT No 82

Communication - Conflict-Resolution - Construction

To provide managers and team leads with a comprehensive framework for managing and navigating sensitive discussions with colleagues who have expressed concerns about them. This framework will include communication techniques, psychological insights, and best practices to ensure an outcome beneficial to both parties involved.

Act as a **Human Resources Expert** with a specialization in **conflict resolution and communication** for the **construction industry**. Could you guide me through a **constructive approach for discussing concerns that a colleague has raised about me**? Please include **conversational frameworks, active listening techniques, and the role of nonverbal communication**. Make sure to cover how **to maintain professionalism and address the issue without escalating it further**. Delve into uncharted territories and groundbreaking concepts to ensure effective communication and problem-solving. Let's dissect this in a structured manner. Write using a **diplomatic** tone and a **how-to** writing style.

Act as a **[profession]** with a specialization in **[area of expertise]** for the **[industry]**. Could you guide me through **[specific challenge/opportunity]**? Please include **[methods/techniques]**. Make sure to cover how **[key areas/topics]**. Delve into uncharted territories and groundbreaking concepts to ensure effective communication and problem-solving. Let's dissect this in a structured manner. Write using a **[type]** tone and **[style]** writing style.

Example 1: Act as a Corporate Trainer with a specialization in emotional intelligence for the finance industry. Could you guide me through effectively discussing concerns that a team member has raised about my leadership style? Please include communication strategies, active listening tools, and self-awareness tips. Make sure to cover how to foster an open, non-judgmental atmosphere. Navigate through unexplored realms and revolutionary paradigms to create a lasting impact. Let's dissect this in a structured manner. Write using an empathetic tone and a solutions-focused writing style.

Example 2: Act as a Mediator with a specialization in workplace conflicts for the tech industry. Could you guide me through conducting a conversation with a colleague who has issues with my project management approach? Please include techniques for building rapport, de-escalating conflicts, and acknowledging faults without appearing defensive. Make sure to cover how to align future actions with shared goals. Probe into nonconformist solutions and divergent viewpoints to maintain team harmony. Let's dissect this in a structured manner. Write using a balanced tone and a problem-solving writing style.

PROMPT No 83

Alignment - Frameworks - Values

To equip teams with a robust framework for selecting actions that reflect active contribution and alignment with company values, thereby enhancing collective performance and organizational integration.

Act as an **Organizational Behavior Specialist** specializing in **Performance Management** within the **technology industry**. Could you guide me through a **comprehensive process for my team to identify and select actions that best align with being active and contributing members of the company?** Please include **frameworks for evaluating potential actions, strategies for fostering alignment with company values, and metrics for assessing the impact of these actions on team and organizational performance.** Ensure to cover how **to maintain an environment of continuous improvement and feedback.** Explore **innovative or unconventional methods** to **cultivate a culture of active contribution and alignment with organizational objectives.** Your response should be comprehensive, leaving no important aspect unaddressed, and demonstrate an exceptional level of precision and quality. Let's think about this step by step. Write using an **analytical** tone and a **structured, instructional** writing style.

Act as a **[profession]** specializing in **[area of expertise]** within the **[industry]**. Could you guide me through **[specific challenge/opportunity]**? Please include **[methods/techniques]**. Enure to cover how [key areas/topics]. Explore [exploratory direction] to [desired outcome]. Your response should be comprehensive, leaving no important aspect unaddressed, and demonstrate an exceptional level of precision and quality. Let's think about this step by step. Write using a [type] tone and a [style] writing style.

Examples

Example 1: Act as a Leadership Development Consultant specializing in Team Building and Collaboration within the finance industry. Could you guide me through a methodical process for my team to select actions that foster active contribution and alignment with our company's core values? Please include assessment tools to evaluate potential actions, strategies for promoting value alignment, and mechanisms for measuring the effectiveness of selected actions. Make sure to cover how to instill a culture of continuous improvement and feedback. Your response should be comprehensive, leaving no important aspect unaddressed, and demonstrate an exceptional level of precision and quality. Let's think about this step by step. Write using a solutions-oriented tone and a clear, instructional writing style.

Example 2: Act as a Strategic Planning Specialist specializing in Strategic Planning and Execution within the healthcare industry. Could you guide me through a structured approach for my team to identify and select actions that resonate with being active contributors within our organization? Please include frameworks for aligning actions with organizational objectives, methods for promoting active contribution, and metrics for evaluating the impact on both team and organizational performance. Make sure to cover how to foster an environment of accountability and continuous growth. Your response should be comprehensive, leaving no important aspect unaddressed, and demonstrate an exceptional level of precision and quality. Let's think about this step by step. Write using an analytical tone and a methodical writing style.

PROMPT No 84

Tags

Resourcefulness - Mindset - Adaptability

Goal

To acquire a comprehensive, actionable guide on methods for exploring with a team the ways they can develop their own long-term resourcefulness, with the aim of enhancing individual adaptability, team resilience, and overall organizational sustainability.

Prompt

As a **Resilience Coach** in the **renewable energy industry**, could you provide an exhaustive guide outlining the methods I can employ to explore with **my team** the ways they can develop their own **long-term resourcefulness**? Please include **mindset-shaping activities**. Segment the guide into **distinct categories**, and substantiate each with **scholarly references**. Explore unconventional approaches and diverse viewpoints. Let's dissect this carefully. Write using an **analytical** tone and a **structured** writing style.

Formula

As a **[profession]** in the **[industry]**, could you provide an exhaustive guide outlining the methods **[I/Name/Role]** can employ to explore with **[my/our/their]** **[team/group/department]** the ways they can develop their own **[long-term resourcefulness/specific quality]**? Please include **[skill-building exercises/mindset-shaping activities]**. Segment the guide into **[distinct categories]**, and substantiate each with **[empirical data/scholarly references]**. Explore unconventional approaches and diverse viewpoints. Let's dissect this carefully. Write using a **[type]** tone and **[style]** writing style.

Example 1: As a Talent Development Specialist in the finance industry, could you provide an exhaustive guide outlining the methods a department head can employ to explore with their analysts the ways they can develop their own long-term resourcefulness? Please include both problem-solving workshops and resilience training. Divide the guide into key areas, and validate each with market studies and peer-reviewed articles. Investigate unexpected avenues and creative pathways. Let's examine each dimension meticulously. Write using a focused tone and a concise writing style.

Example 2: As a Leadership Development Consultant in the education sector, could you provide an exhaustive guide outlining the methods I can employ to explore with my faculty the ways they can develop their own long-term resourcefulness? Please include both pedagogical skills training and emotional intelligence exercises. Break the guide into actionable steps, and corroborate each with educational benchmarks and case studies. Unearth hidden gems and non-traditional methods. Let's tackle this in a phased manner. Write using a balanced tone and a nuanced writing style.

PROMPT No 85

Emotional-Intelligence - Cohesive - Resilience

To foster awareness and understanding within a team regarding how emotions and feelings can influence decision-making, particularly during challenging or high-pressure situations. This self-awareness aims to enhance emotional intelligence, encourage thoughtful response rather than reactive decisions, and contribute to a more cohesive and effective team dynamic.

Act as an **Emotional Intelligence Coach** specializing in the **renewable energy industry**. Could you help **my team and me to recognize and understand our feelings or emotions that may be affecting our decision-making process when dealing with a challenging situation at work**? Insight into this area is crucial for **enhancing our collective emotional intelligence, improving our problem-solving abilities, and creating a more empathetic and resilient team environment**. Please provide an in-depth response that includes **techniques for self-awareness, team-building activities, emotional intelligence assessments, and strategies for mindful decision-making**. Let's explore this step by step. Write using an **empathetic** tone and **instructive** writing style.

Act as an **[profession]** specializing in the **[industry]**. Could you help **[contextual challenge/opportunity]**? Insight into this area is crucial for **[desired outcome]**. Please provide an in-depth response that includes **[specific components or methods]**. Let's explore this step by step. Write using a **[type]** tone and **[style]** writing style.

Example 1: Act as a Team Dynamics Specialist specializing in the aerospace & defense industry. Could you guide my resarch & development team to become more aware of their emotional triggers and biases affecting their decision-making in complex cases? Understanding this dynamic is vital for maintaining objectivity, enhancing collaboration, and navigating stressful situations effectively. Please craft a multifaceted response that considers individual emotional profiles, group workshops, mindfulness practices, and ongoing reflective exercises. Let's dissect this carefully. Write using a respectful tone and analytical writing style.

Example 2: Act as a Leadership Development Consultant specializing in the manufacturing industry. Could you assist my management team and me in recognizing how our emotions may influence our decisions during crisis management? Gaining this awareness is essential for fostering strong leadership, boosting problem-solving efficiency, and sustaining a harmonious team culture. Please design a comprehensive response that integrates emotional intelligence assessments, scenario-based training, meditation techniques, and peer feedback mechanisms. Let's analyze this piece by piece. Write using an encouraging tone and engaging writing style.

PROMPT No 86

Engagement - Productivity - Mindfulness

To adeptly devise and implement strategies that rejuvenate team engagement and presence, ensuring a conducive atmosphere for enhanced productivity, communication, and collective achievement.

Act as an **Engagement Revitalization Expert** specializing in **Mindful Leadership** within the **software development industry**. Could you guide me through **robust strategies to steer my team back to full presence whenever I discern a lapse in their engagement**? Please include **diagnostic tools to ascertain the level of engagement, mindfulness practices, and re-engagement techniques**. Ensure to cover how **to foster a culture of sustained presence and attentiveness**. Delve into avant-garde or pioneering strategies that could provide a fresh impetus to team engagement. Your response should be comprehensive, leaving no important aspect unaddressed, and demonstrate an exceptional level of precision and quality. Let's think about this step by step. Write using a **focused** tone and a **step-by-step instructional** writing style.

Act as a **[profession]** specializing in **[area of expertise]** within the **[industry]**. Could you guide me through **[specific challenge/opportunity]**? Please include **[methods/techniques]**. Ensure to cover how

[key areas/topics]. Delve into avant-garde or pioneering strategies that could provide a fresh impetus to team engagement. Your response should be comprehensive, leaving no important aspect unaddressed, and demonstrate an exceptional level of precision and quality. Let's think about this step by step. Write using a **[type]** tone and a **[style]** writing style.

Examples

Example 1: Act as a Team Dynamics Specialist specializing in Engaged Leadership within the financial services industry. Could you guide me through effective strategies to regain full presence and active participation from my team whenever I observe dwindling engagement? Please include engagement assessment tools, interactive activities, and communication best practices. Make sure to cover how to instill a continual sense of presence and enthusiasm among team members. Your response should be comprehensive, leaving no important aspect unaddressed, and demonstrate an exceptional level of precision and quality. Let's think about this step by step. Write using an encouraging tone and a detailed instructional writing style.

Example 2: Act as a Mindful Team Building Advisor specializing in Sustainable Engagement within the hospitality industry. Could you guide me through innovative strategies to rekindle full presence and engagement within my team when I perceive a lapse? Please include mindfulness techniques, feedback loops, and motivational incentives. Make sure to cover how to create a supportive environment that promotes ongoing engagement and attentiveness. Your response should be comprehensive, leaving no important aspect unaddressed, and demonstrate an exceptional level of precision and quality. Let's think about this step by step. Write using a supportive tone and a clear, instructional writing style.

PROMPT No 87

Tags

Resource Management - Utilization - Analytical Guide

Goal

To acquire a comprehensive, actionable guide on methods for identifying how a team can best utilize their existing resources to navigate current challenges, with the aim of enhancing problem-solving capabilities and operational efficiency.

Prompt

As a **Resource Management Expert** in the **logistics industry**, could you provide an exhaustive guide outlining the strategies **my team** and **I** can employ to identify how to utilize our current resources to navigate **our existing challenges**? Please include both **quantitative assessments and qualitative observations**. Segment the guide into **distinct categories**, and substantiate each with **empirical data and scholarly references**. Explore unconventional approaches and diverse viewpoints. Let's dissect this carefully. Write using an **analytical** tone and a **structured** writing style.

Formula

As a **[profession]** in the **[industry]**, could you provide an exhaustive guide outlining the strategies **[I/Name/Role]** and **[my/our/their]** **[team/group/department]** can employ to identify how to utilize our current resources to navigate **[current challenges/specific issues]**? Please include both **[quantitative assessments/qualitative observations]**. Segment the guide into **[distinct categories]**, and substantiate each with **[empirical data/scholarly references]**. Explore unconventional approaches and diverse viewpoints. Let's dissect this carefully. Write using a **[type]** tone and **[style]** writing style.

Example 1: As a Business Strategy Consultant in the healthcare industry, could you provide an exhaustive guide outlining the strategies a medical team and their manager can employ to identify how to utilize their current equipment and staff to navigate patient care challenges? Please include both cost-benefit analyses and staff interviews. Divide the guide into key areas, and validate each with clinical studies and peer-reviewed articles. Investigate unexpected avenues and creative pathways. Let's examine each dimension meticulously. Write using a focused tone and a concise writing style.

Example 2: As a Leadership Development Consultant in the retail sector, could you provide an exhaustive guide outlining the strategies my sales team and I can employ to identify how to utilize our current inventory and floor space to navigate customer engagement challenges? Please include both inventory turnover rates and customer feedback. Break the guide into actionable steps, and corroborate each with industry benchmarks and case studies. Unearth hidden gems and non-traditional methods. Let's tackle this in a phased manner. Write using a balanced tone and a nuanced writing style.

SELF-ASSESSMENT

PROMPT No 88

Presentation - Development - Consulting

To acquire a comprehensive, actionable guide on creating the optimal conditions that will enable a team to plan and take the first step toward enhancing their presentation skills, with the aim of improving communication effectiveness and professional development.

As a **Professional Development Expert** in the **consulting industry**, could you provide an exhaustive guide outlining the conditions I need to create for **my team** to plan to take the first step in enhancing their **presentation skills**? Please include both **environmental factors and motivational strategies**. Segment the guide into **distinct categories**, and substantiate each with **empirical data and scholarly references**. Explore unconventional approaches and diverse viewpoints. Let's dissect this carefully. Write using an **analytical** tone and a **structured** writing style.

As a **[profession]** in the **[industry]**, could you provide an exhaustive guide outlining the conditions **[I/Name/Role]** need to create for **[my/our/their]** **[team/group/department]** to plan to take the first step in enhancing their [skillset]? Please include both **[environmental factors/motivational strategies]**. Segment the guide into **[distinct categories]**, and substantiate each with **[empirical data/scholarly references]**. Explore unconventional approaches and diverse viewpoints. Let's dissect this carefully. Write using a **[type]** tone and **[style]** writing style.

Example 1: As a Communication Coach in the healthcare industry, could you provide an exhaustive guide outlining the conditions a department head needs to create for their nursing staff to plan to take the first step in enhancing their patient communication skills? Please include both workspace adjustments and incentive programs. Divide the guide into key areas, and validate each with clinical studies and peer-reviewed articles. Investigate unexpected avenues and creative pathways. Let's examine each dimension meticulously. Write using a focused tone and a concise writing style.

Example 2: As a Leadership Development Consultant in the technology sector, could you provide an exhaustive guide outlining the conditions I need to create for my software development team to plan to take the first step in enhancing their technical presentation skills? Please include both online resources and team-building exercises. Break the guide into actionable steps, and corroborate each with industry benchmarks and case studies. Unearth hidden gems and non-traditional methods. Let's tackle this in a phased manner. Write using a balanced tone and a nuanced writing style.

PROMPT No 89

Accountability - Success - Analysis

To provide leaders and professionals with a nuanced framework for effectively analyzing and articulating recent professional successes or failures, thereby fostering a culture of accountability, learning, and continuous improvement.

Act as a **Career Development Coach** specializing in the **finance sector**. Could you elucidate the **key elements** that **professionals** should consider when **describing** their **recent successes** in the **workplace**? Include **both qualitative and quantitative metrics, psychological factors, and organizational context** that **should** be **considered**. Let's methodically dissect each component. Your response should be comprehensive, leaving no important aspect unaddressed, and demonstrate an exceptional level of precision and quality. Write using an **analytical** tone and a **structured** writing style.

Act as a **[profession]** specializing in the **[industry]**. Could you elucidate the **[key/critical/essential]** elements that **[professionals/individuals/team members]** should consider when **[describing/analyzing/evaluating]** their **[recent/past/current]** **[successes/failures]** in the [workplace/professional setting]? Include [both qualitative and quantitative metrics/psychological factors/organizational context] that [should/must/could] be [considered/taken into account]. Let's methodically dissect each component. Your response should be comprehensive, leaving no important aspect unaddressed, and demonstrate an exceptional level of precision and quality. Write using a [type] tone and [style] writing style.

Example 1: Act as a Performance Analyst specializing in the technology sector. Could you outline the critical elements that engineers should consider when evaluating their recent project successes or failures? Include KPIs, team dynamics, and client feedback as part of the evaluation. Let's sequentially address each element. Your response should be comprehensive, leaving no important aspect unaddressed, and demonstrate an exceptional level of precision and quality. Write using a data-driven tone and an informative writing style.

Example 2: Act as a Leadership Consultant specializing in the healthcare industry. Could you delineate the essential factors that medical professionals should consider when analyzing their recent successes or failures in patient care? Include patient satisfaction scores, peer reviews, and internal audits. Let's tackle this in a phased manner. Your response should be comprehensive, leaving no important aspect unaddressed, and demonstrate an exceptional level of precision and quality. Write using an empathetic tone and a consultative writing style.

PROMPT No 90

Data - Collaboration - Continuous-improvement

To empower teams with a clear, systematic, and insightful methodology for identifying relevant metrics and assessment techniques that accurately measure progress towards their defined goals, fostering a culture of continuous improvement and goal attainment.

Act as a **Performance Measurement Specialist** specializing in **Goal Progression Metrics** within the **technology sector.** Could you guide me through **comprehensive approaches for my team to elucidate on their own how to measure progress towards their goals?** Please include **metric identification, key performance indicators (KPIs) development, and data analysis techniques.** Make sure to cover how **to foster a collaborative environment that encourages continuous feedback and refinement of measurement strategies. Explore innovative or under-utilized methods to offer a fresh perspective on progress measurement.** Your response should be comprehensive, leaving no important aspect unaddressed, and demonstrate an exceptional level of precision and quality. Let's think about this step by step. Write using a **precise** tone and a **systematic, instructional** writing style.

Act as a [profession] specializing in [area of expertise] within the [industry]. Could you guide me through [specific challenge/opportunity]? Please include [methods/techniques]. Make sure to cover how [key areas/topics]. Explore [exploratory direction] to [desired outcome]. Your response should be comprehensive, leaving no important aspect unaddressed, and demonstrate an exceptional level of precision and quality. Let's think about this step by step. Write using a [type] tone and a [style] writing style.

Example 1: Act as a Performance Analytics Advisor specializing in Goal Achievement Metrics within the financial sector. Could you guide me through structured approaches for my team to self-clarify how they can measure progress towards their goals? Please include the development of relevant KPIs, utilization of analytics tools, and the establishment of regular progress review sessions. Make sure to cover how to inculcate a culture of data-driven decision making. Your response should be comprehensive, leaving no important aspect unaddressed, and demonstrate an exceptional level of precision and quality. Let's think about this step by step. Write using an analytical tone and a detailed, instructional writing style.

Example 2: Act as a Goal Setting and Measurement Expert specializing in Progress Tracking Techniques within the healthcare sector. Could you guide me through effective methods for my team to independently discern how to measure progress towards their goals? Please include goal alignment workshops, metric brainstorming sessions, and feedback loop establishment. Make sure to cover how to encourage team ownership of the measurement process. Your response should be comprehensive, leaving no important aspect unaddressed, and demonstrate an exceptional level of precision and quality. Let's think about this step by step. Write using a collaborative tone and a step-by-step instructional writing style.

SKILLS

PROMPT No 91

Motivation - Skills - Optimization

To gain a nuanced understanding of the skills that motivate and uplift your team, aiming to further optimize these elements for enhanced team performance and morale.

As an **HR manager** specializing in **talent development** within the **healthcare industry**, provide an exhaustive and meticulous examination, incorporating innovative insights and inventive strategies for **reflecting** on the skills that **energize** and **inspire** your team as they **utilize** them. Explore strategies to **make the most of** these skills in **day-to-day operations and project management**.

As a **[profession]** specializing in **[area of expertise/focus]** within the **[industry]**, provide an exhaustive and meticulous examination, incorporating innovative insights and inventive strategies for **[reflecting/contemplating/considering]** on the skills that **[energize/motivate/invigorate]** and **[inspire/uplift/empower]** your team as they **[utilize/employ/use]** them. Explore strategies to **[optimize/maximize/leverage]** these skills in **[day-to-day operations/project management/team initiatives]**.

Example 1: As a team leader specializing in product management within the retail industry, provide an exhaustive and meticulous examination, incorporating innovative insights and inventive strategies for contemplating the skills that motivate and uplift your sales team as they employ them. Explore strategies to maximize these skills in team initiatives.

Example 2: As a coach specializing in executive leadership within the nonprofit sector, provide an exhaustive and meticulous examination, incorporating innovative insights and inventive strategies for considering the skills that invigorate and empower your board of directors as they use them. Explore strategies to optimize these skills in day-to-day operations.

PROMPT No 92

Leadership - Feedback - Development

To proficiently assist a supervisor in identifying and honing new skills requisite for heightened effectiveness, fostering a mutually beneficial relationship, and contributing to organizational excellence.

Act as a **Leadership Enhancement Specialist** specializing in **Executive Skill Development** within the **hospitality industry**. Could you guide me through a **tactful and systematic approach to help my boss identify the new skills they need to improve and become more effective in**? Please include **tools for skill identification, techniques for constructive feedback, and methods for supporting skill development**. Make sure to cover how **to maintain a respectful and supportive demeanor while addressing areas for improvement**. Explore **subtle and motivational methods** to **encourage the willingness for self-improvement**. Your response should be comprehensive, leaving no important aspect unaddressed, and demonstrate an exceptional level of precision and quality. Let's think about this step by step. Write using a **respectful** tone and a **tactful, encouraging** writing style.

Act as a **[profession]** specializing in **[area of expertise]** within the **[industry]**. Could you guide me through **[specific challenge/opportunity]**? Please include **[methods/techniques]**. Make sure to cover how **[key areas/topics]**. Explore **[exploratory direction]** to **[desired outcome]**. Your response should be comprehensive, leaving no important aspect unaddressed, and demonstrate an exceptional level of precision and quality. Let's think about this step by step. Write using a **[type]** tone and a **[style]** writing style.

Examples

Example 1: Act as an Executive Coaching Expert specializing in Skill Augmentation within the healthcare sector. Could you guide me through a diplomatic method to assist my supervisor in identifying and enhancing the new skills required for greater effectiveness? Please include diagnostic assessments, feedback delivery techniques, and coaching methodologies. Make sure to cover how to establish a trust-based rapport to facilitate open communication. Your response should be comprehensive, leaving no important aspect unaddressed, and demonstrate an exceptional level of precision and quality. Let's think about this step by step. Write using a supportive tone and a detail-oriented, instructional writing style.

Example 2: Act as a Leadership Development Advisor specializing in Constructive Feedback within the real estate sector. Could you guide me through a structured strategy to aid my boss in pinpointing and refining the new skills necessary for enhanced effectiveness? Please include self-assessment tools, 360-degree feedback mechanisms, and individual development plans. Make sure to cover how to maintain a positive and constructive atmosphere during this process. Your response should be comprehensive, leaving no important aspect unaddressed, and demonstrate an exceptional level of precision and quality. Let's think about this step by step. Write using a collaborative tone and a facilitative, step-by-step writing style.

STRATEGIES

PROMPT No 93

Tags

Innovation - Experimentation - Creativity

Goal

To identify innovative methodologies and frameworks that empower you and your team to explore new behaviors, thoughts, or approaches for enhanced problem-solving and creativity.

Prompt

As a **project manager** specializing in **software development** within the **technology industry**, provide an exhaustive and meticulous examination, incorporating innovative insights and inventive strategies for **identifying** various avenues to **experiment** with new **behaviors, thoughts, or approaches**. Discuss how these could **benefit problem-solving** and **creativity** in the team.

Formula

As a **[profession]** specializing in **[area of expertise/focus]** within the **[industry]**, provide an exhaustive and meticulous examination, incorporating innovative insights and inventive strategies for **[identifying/listing/uncovering]** various avenues to **[experiment/test/engage]** with new **[behaviors/thoughts/approaches]**. Discuss how these could **[benefit/enhance/improve]** **[problem-solving/creativity/team performance]** in the team.

Example 1: As a research director specializing in behavioral science within the education sector, provide an exhaustive and meticulous examination, incorporating innovative insights and inventive strategies for listing various avenues to test new behaviors, thoughts, or approaches. Discuss how these could improve creativity in the academic staff.

Example 2: As an HR consultant specializing in organizational culture within the manufacturing industry, provide an exhaustive and meticulous examination, incorporating innovative insights and inventive strategies for uncovering various avenues to engage with new behaviors, thoughts, or approaches. Discuss how these could enhance problem-solving among factory workers.

STRENGTH

PROMPT No 94

Tags

Top-strengths - Progress - Motivation

Goal

To equip leaders with a robust framework that enables their teams to engage in reflective practices, focusing on identifying and leveraging their top three to five career strengths for further professional growth and development.

Prompt

Act as a **Career Development Specialist** specializing in the **manufacturing industry**. Could you **provide** a **structured methodology** for **facilitating** team **reflection** on the **top three to five strengths** they **most frequently utilize** in their **careers**, and how these could be **leveraged for further progress**? Include **actionable exercises and validated assessment tools**. Let's systematically explore each facet. Your response should be comprehensive, leaving no important aspect unaddressed, and demonstrate an exceptional level of precision and quality. Write using a **motivational** tone and a **solution-oriented** writing style.

Formula

Act as a **[profession]** specializing in the **[industry]**. Could you **[provide/outline/design]** a **[structured/comprehensive/step-by-step]** **[methodology/framework/approach]** for **[facilitating/guiding/enabling]** team **[reflection/analysis/evaluation]** on the **[top/most critical/most impactful]** **[three to five/number]** **[strengths/skills/abilities]** they **[most frequently/often/regularly]** **[utilize/employ/leverage]** in their **[careers/professional lives/job roles]**, and how these could be **[leveraged/utilized/employed]** for **[further/additional/ongoing]** **[progress/growth/development]**? Include **[actionable/practical/effective]** **[exercises/activities/assessment tools]**. Let's systematically explore each facet. Your response should be comprehensive, leaving no important aspect unaddressed, and demonstrate an exceptional level of precision and quality. Write using a **[type]** tone and **[style]** writing style.

Examples

Example 1: Act as a Leadership Coach specializing in the tech industry. Could you outline a comprehensive approach for helping my software engineering team reflect on the top three to five skills they frequently employ in their roles, and how to leverage these for career advancement? Include practical exercises and peer-review mechanisms. Let's examine each dimension meticulously. Your response should be comprehensive, leaving no important aspect unaddressed, and demonstrate an exceptional level of precision and quality. Write using an analytical tone and a data-driven writing style.

Example 2: Act as an Organizational Development Consultant specializing in the healthcare sector. Could you design a step-by-step framework for guiding my medical staff in identifying the top three to five strengths they use in patient care, and how these can be further developed? Include validated psychometric assessments and real-world scenarios. Let's deconstruct this subject stepwise. Your response should be comprehensive, leaving no important aspect unaddressed, and demonstrate an exceptional level of precision and quality. Write using an empathetic tone and a patient-centered writing style.

PROMPT No 95

Tags

Scrutinizing - Strengths - Patterns

Goal

To equip leaders with a robust methodology for scrutinizing the list of strengths within their team, thereby identifying recurring patterns that can be leveraged for strategic decision-making, team development, and performance optimization.

Prompt

Act as an **Organizational Development Consultant** specializing in the **e-commerce industry**. Could you **elucidate** the **best practices** for **examining** the **list** of **strengths** within **my** team and **identifying** any **recurring patterns**? Include **data analytics techniques, qualitative assessments, and team dynamics theories**. Let's systematically explore each facet. Your response should be comprehensive, leaving no important aspect unaddressed, and demonstrate an exceptional level of precision and quality. Write using an **analytical** tone and a **methodical** writing style.

Formula

Act as a **[profession]** specializing in the **[industry]**. Could you **[elucidate/explain/outline]** the **[best practices/optimal methods/effective strategies]** for **[examining/scrutinizing/analyzing]** the **[list/collection/array]** of **[strengths/skills/talents]** within **[my/our/the]** team and **[identifying/detecting/uncovering]** any **[recurring/repeated/common]** **[patterns/trends/themes]**? Include **[data analytics techniques/qualitative assessments/team dynamics theories/psychometric tests]**. Let's systematically explore each facet. Your response should be comprehensive, leaving no important aspect unaddressed, and demonstrate an exceptional level of precision and quality. Write using a **[type]** tone and **[style]** writing style.

Examples

Example 1: Act as a Talent Management Specialist specializing in the healthcare industry. Could you explain the best practices for scrutinizing the list of skills within my nursing team and identifying any common trends? Include statistical analysis, peer reviews, and behavioral assessments. Let's carefully evaluate each segment. Write using a data-driven tone and an evidence-based writing style. Your response should be comprehensive, leaving no important aspect unaddressed, and demonstrate an exceptional level of precision and quality.

Example 2: Act as a Leadership Development Advisor specializing in the aerospace industry. Could you outline the optimal methods for analyzing the array of talents within my engineering team and detecting any repeated themes? Include machine learning algorithms, 360-degree feedback, and organizational psychology theories. Let's delve into each aspect with precision. Write using a strategic tone and a research-oriented writing style. Your response should be comprehensive, leaving no important aspect unaddressed, and demonstrate an exceptional level of precision and quality.

PROMPT No 96

Growth   - Strengths - Development

To equip individuals with a reflective and analytical approach to keenly observe, understand, and leverage their inherent strengths, thereby fostering self-awareness, continuous learning, and personal and professional development.

Act as a **Personal Development Consultant** specializing in **Strengths-Based Self-Assessment** within the **healthcare industry.** Could you guide me through **the key considerations and methodologies to meticulously observe and reflect on any notable observations about my own strengths?** Please include **self-assessment tools, reflective exercises, and frameworks for analyzing and leveraging observed strengths.** Make sure to cover how to **maintain a growth mindset and how to actionably apply these insights for continuous personal and professional development.** Venture into innovative and perhaps unconventional strategies to deepen self-awareness and enhance strengths utilization. Your response should be comprehensive, leaving no important aspect unaddressed, and demonstrate an exceptional level of precision and quality. Let's think about this step by step. Write using an **insightful** tone and a **structured, actionable** writing style.

Act as a **[profession]** specializing in **[area of expertise]** within the **[industry]**. Could you guide me through **[specific challenge/opportunity]**? Please include **[methods/techniques]**. Make sure to cover how **[key areas/topics]**. Venture into innovative and perhaps unconventional strategies to deepen self-awareness and enhance strengths utilization. Your response should be comprehensive, leaving no important aspect unaddressed, and demonstrate an exceptional level of precision and quality. Let's think about this step by step. Write using a **[type]** tone and a **[style]** writing style.

Example 1: Act as a Self-Development Coach specializing in Reflective Practice within the education sector. Could you guide me through a systematic approach to keenly observe and reflect on my strengths, especially as they manifest in my professional interactions? Please include observational techniques, self-reflection frameworks, and actionable steps to enhance these strengths further. Make sure to cover how to create a conducive environment for continuous self-reflection and learning. Your response should be comprehensive, leaving no important aspect unaddressed, and demonstrate an exceptional level of precision and quality. Let's think about this step by step. Write using an encouraging tone and a step-by-step writing style.

Example 2: Act as a Career Development Advisor specializing in Strengths Identification within the financial sector. Could you guide me through a comprehensive methodology to observe, analyze, and reflect on my own strengths, especially in high-pressure situations? Please include emotional intelligence tools, stress management techniques, and strategies for leveraging strengths in challenging scenarios. Make sure to cover how to maintain a balanced perspective and a proactive approach towards personal growth. Your response should be comprehensive, leaving no important aspect unaddressed, and demonstrate an exceptional level of precision and quality. Let's think about this step by step. Write using an analytical tone and a structured, forward-thinking writing style.

PROMPT № 97

Tags
Evaluation - Strengths - Allocation

Goal
To equip leaders with a nuanced and actionable guide for facilitating team reflections focused on the active utilization of individual strengths, aiming to enhance self-awareness, team cohesion, and overall performance.

Prompt
Act as a **Team Dynamics Expert** specializing in the **manufacturing industry**. Could you delineate a **structured** methodology for facilitating a **reflection session** with my team on the **outcomes and experiences** they **encounter** when **actively employing** one of their **strengths**? Include **specific questions to ask, psychological theories that support this type of reflection**, and **potential metrics for evaluating its effectiveness**. Let's think about this step by step. Write using a **consultative** tone and an **advisory** writing style.

Formula
Act as a [profession] specializing in the [industry]. Could you delineate a [structured/comprehensive/methodical] methodology for facilitating a [reflection session/group discussion/team meeting] with my team on the [outcomes/experiences/impacts] they [encounter/observe/realize] when [actively employing/utilizing/leveraging] one of their [strengths/skills/talents]? Include [specific questions/targeted queries/guiding prompts], [supporting psychological theories/relevant frameworks], and [potential metrics/KPIs/evaluation criteria] for [measuring/assessing/evaluating] its [effectiveness/impact/success]. Let's think about this step by step. Write using a [type] tone and [style] writing style.

Example 1: Act as a Corporate Trainer specializing in the retail sector. Could you outline a comprehensive strategy for facilitating a reflection session with my sales team on the experiences they have when leveraging their communication skills? Include targeted questions, relevant psychological theories like Positive Psychology, and key performance indicators for assessing impact. Let's systematically explore each facet. Write using a growth-oriented tone and expansion-minded writing style.

Example 2: Act as an Organizational Psychologist specializing in the non-profit sector. Could you provide a methodical approach for facilitating a group discussion with my team on the outcomes they realize when actively using their problem-solving skills? Include guiding prompts, theories such as Strengths-Based Leadership, and potential metrics for success evaluation. Let's carefully evaluate each segment. Write using a quality-focused tone and meticulous writing style.

PROMPT No 98

Overleveraging - Performance - Adaptation

To facilitate reflective exploration among my team on the implications of overleveraging strengths, aiming to balance optimal strength utilization with avoiding over-extension to enhance individual and collective performance.

As a **Performance Management Specialist** within the **Business Consulting industry**, how can I meticulously facilitate a reflective exploration among my team regarding the impact of extending their strengths to the extreme on their **performance and the resultant outcomes**? I am seeking a robust discussion that unravels **actionable strategies, potential repercussions, and adaptive measures** to ensure an **optimal utilization** of strengths that contributes to **enhanced performance**, without veering into over-extension. This discussion should also delve into the broader ramifications this understanding might have on **team dynamics, organizational culture, and client satisfaction**, ensuring a thorough analysis with an exceptional level of precision and quality.

As a **[Profession]** within the **[Industry]**, how can I meticulously facilitate a reflective exploration among my team regarding the impact of extending their strengths to the extreme on their **[performance/outcomes/other relevant areas]**? I am seeking a robust discussion that unravels **[actionable strategies/potential repercussions/adaptive measures]** to ensure an [optimal utilization/balanced approach] of strengths that contributes to **[enhanced performance/sustainable success/other relevant outcomes]**, without veering into over-extension. This discussion should also delve into the broader ramifications this understanding might have on **[team dynamics/organizational culture/client satisfaction or other relevant impact areas]**, ensuring a thorough analysis with an exceptional level of precision and quality.

Example 1: As a Talent Development Lead within the Technology Sector, how can I meticulously facilitate a reflective exploration among my team regarding the impact of extending their strengths to the extreme on their project delivery and client satisfaction? I am seeking a robust discussion that unravels actionable strategies, potential repercussions, and adaptive measures to ensure an optimal utilization of strengths that contributes to enhanced project outcomes, without veering into over-extension. This discussion should also delve into the broader ramifications this understanding might have on team collaboration, innovation culture, and client relations, ensuring a thorough analysis with an exceptional level of precision and quality.

Example 2: As a Performance Optimization Analyst within the Healthcare Sector, how can I meticulously facilitate a reflective exploration among my clinical team regarding the impact of extending their strengths to the extreme on patient care and overall operational efficiency? I am seeking a robust discussion that unravels actionable strategies, potential repercussions, and adaptive measures to ensure an optimal utilization of strengths that contributes to enhanced patient outcomes, without veering into over-extension. This discussion should also delve into the broader ramifications this understanding might have on interdisciplinary collaboration, organizational culture, and patient satisfaction, ensuring a thorough analysis with an exceptional level of precision and quality.

PROMPT No 99

Tags
Rejuvenation - Alignment - Assessment
Goal
To devise a meticulous process for reflecting on and addressing instances where team members possess strengths that they no longer enjoy utilizing, thereby fostering a rejuvenated engagement and alignment between personal satisfaction and organizational effectiveness.
Prompt
Act as a **Work Fulfillment Analyst** specializing in **Employee Engagement and Satisfaction** within the **manufacturing industry**. Could you guide me through **the most optimal process to reflect on any strengths my team possesses that they no longer enjoy using**? Please include **assessment tools, reflective exercises, and dialogic strategies**. Ensure to cover how **to realign these strengths with job roles in a manner that rejuvenates enjoyment and enhances productivity**. Investigate **both conventional wisdom and novel approaches to rediscovering job satisfaction through strengths alignment**. Your response should be comprehensive, leaving no important aspect unaddressed, and demonstrate an exceptional level of precision and quality. Let's think about this step by step. Write using a **motivational** tone and a **strategic** writing style.
Formula
Act as a [profession] specializing in [area of expertise] within the [industry]. Could you guide me through [specific challenge/opportunity]? Please include [methods/techniques]. Ensure to cover how [key areas/topics]. Investigate [additional exploration]. Your response should be comprehensive,

leaving no important aspect unaddressed, and demonstrate an exceptional level of precision and quality. Let's think about this step by step. Write using a **[type]** tone and a **[style]** writing style.

Example 1: Act as a Professional Development Consultant specializing in Job Role Alignment within the healthcare sector. Could you guide me through the most effective process to explore any strengths my team possesses but have grown weary of using? Please include evaluation mechanisms, reflection sessions, and job redesign strategies. Ensure to cover how to reignite the passion for utilizing these strengths in a manner beneficial to both the individuals and the organization. Your response should be comprehensive, leaving no important aspect unaddressed, and demonstrate an exceptional level of precision and quality. Let's think about this step by step. Write using an inspiring tone and a solution-oriented writing style.

Example 2: Act as a Career Satisfaction Specialist specializing in Strengths Re-engagement within the education sector. Could you guide me through a thorough process to identify and address strengths my team possesses but no longer find enjoyable to utilize? Please include diagnostic surveys, facilitated discussions, and actionable plans for re-engagement. Ensure to cover how to foster a culture that continuously aligns strengths with job satisfaction and organizational goals. Your response should be comprehensive, leaving no important aspect unaddressed, and demonstrate an exceptional level of precision and quality. Let's think about this step by step. Write using an empathetic tone and a transformation-focused writing style.

PROMPT No 100

Ideation - Implementation - Engagement

To devise and implement insightful actions that will significantly enhance the alignment between team members' roles and their inherent strengths, thereby promoting job satisfaction, improving performance, and fostering a productive and harmonious work environment.

Act as a **Strengths-Based Development Strategist** with a specialization in **Role Alignment** within the **healthcare industry**. Could you guide me through **innovative ideas and actionable strategies to enhance the alignment between my team's roles and their strengths?** Please include **a thorough analysis of existing roles and strengths, ideation techniques,** and a **step-by-step action plan for implementing alignment strategies.** Make sure to cover how **to engage team members in this process, and ways to measure and sustain the alignment over time.** Venture into **pioneering concepts and solutions that may defy traditional approaches to role allocation and strengths utilization.** Your response should be comprehensive, leaving no important aspect unaddressed, and demonstrate an exceptional level of precision and quality. Let's think about this step by step. Write using a **solution-oriented** tone and a **forward-thinking** writing style.

Act as a **[profession]** with a specialization in **[area of expertise]** within the **[industry]**. Could you guide me through **[specific challenge/opportunity]**? Please include **[methods/techniques]**. Make sure to cover how **[key areas/topics]**. Venture into **[additional exploration]**. Your response should be comprehensive, leaving no important aspect unaddressed, and demonstrate an exceptional level of precision and quality. Let's think about this step by step. Write using a **[type]** tone and a **[style]** writing style.

Example 1: Act as a Talent Optimization Consultant with a specialization in Strengths-Based Leadership within the technology sector. Could you guide me through pioneering ideas and pragmatic actions to enhance the alignment between my team's roles and their strengths? Please include a diagnostic assessment of current role-strengths alignment, brainstorming sessions, and a structured implementation plan. Make sure to cover how to create a continuous feedback loop for monitoring and refining this alignment. Venture into avant-garde strategies that might challenge conventional role definitions and strengths utilization. Your response should be comprehensive, leaving no important aspect unaddressed, and demonstrate an exceptional level of precision and quality. Let's think about this step by step. Write using an innovative tone and a strategic writing style.

Example 2: Act as an Organizational Development Specialist with a specialization in Strengths Alignment within the manufacturing sector. Could you guide me through creative ideas and actionable steps to enhance the alignment between my team's roles and their strengths? Please include situational analysis techniques, collaborative ideation sessions, and a phased action plan for realignment. Make sure to cover how to instill a culture of strengths recognition and utilization amongst team members. Explore groundbreaking methodologies that may redefine traditional approaches to role assignment and strengths leverage. Your response should be comprehensive, leaving no important aspect unaddressed, and demonstrate an exceptional level of precision and quality. Let's think about this step by step. Write using an engaging tone and a practical writing style.

SUPPORT

PROMPT No 101

Focus - Alignment - Productivity

To meticulously develop and implement a comprehensive strategy that fosters a conducive environment for my team to maintain a steadfast focus on overarching organizational objectives and specific tasks, optimizing productivity and alignment with the strategic vision.

As a **Team Cohesion Strategist** specializing in **Vision Alignment** within the **Management Consulting industry**, how can I methodically develop and implement a well-rounded strategy to create a conducive environment for my team to consistently maintain focus on the broader organizational goals while also effectively addressing specific tasks at hand? I seek an extensive discourse on a structured approach encompassing actionable methods, tools, and best practices to promote a culture of **focused engagement**, ensuring alignment with **strategic objectives**. Additionally, the discourse should articulate the consequential impact of such an approach on **team productivity, organizational alignment, and stakeholder satisfaction**, encapsulating every pivotal aspect with an exceptional degree of precision and quality.

As a **[Profession]** specializing in **[Specialization]** within the **[Industry]**, how can I methodically develop and implement a well-rounded strategy to create a conducive environment for my team to consistently maintain focus on the broader organizational goals while also effectively addressing specific tasks at hand? I seek an extensive discourse on a structured approach encompassing actionable methods, tools, and best practices to promote a culture of **[Focused Engagement/Other Relevant Aspect]**, ensuring alignment with **[Strategic Objectives/Other Relevant Objective]**. Additionally, the discourse should articulate the consequential impact of such an approach on **[Team Productivity/Organizational Alignment/Stakeholder Satisfaction or Other Relevant Outcome]**, encapsulating every pivotal aspect with an exceptional degree of precision and quality.

Example 1: As a Collaborative Efficacy Expert specializing in Goal-Oriented Focus within the Digital Marketing industry, how can I methodically develop and implement a well-rounded strategy to create a conducive environment for my team to consistently maintain focus on the broader organizational goals while also effectively addressing specific tasks at hand? I seek an extensive discourse on a structured approach encompassing actionable methods, tools, and best practices to promote a culture of targeted engagement, ensuring alignment with campaign objectives. Additionally, the discourse should articulate the consequential impact of such an approach on campaign effectiveness, client satisfaction, and competitive positioning, encapsulating every pivotal aspect with an exceptional degree of precision and quality.

Example 2: As a Strategic Concentration Architect specializing in Task Prioritization within the Healthcare Management industry, how can I methodically develop and implement a well-rounded strategy to create a conducive environment for my team to consistently maintain focus on the broader organizational goals while also effectively addressing specific tasks at hand? I seek an extensive discourse on a structured approach encompassing actionable methods, tools, and best practices to promote a culture of disciplined focus, ensuring alignment with patient care standards. Additionally, the discourse should articulate the consequential impact of such an approach on patient satisfaction, regulatory compliance, and operational efficiency, encapsulating every pivotal aspect with an exceptional degree of precision and quality.

PROMPT No 102

Hindrances - Progression - Feedback

To decipher what hindrances or obsolete practices my team needs to discard to foster a more robust progression or forward momentum, thereby achieving higher efficiency and effectiveness in meeting our objectives.

Act as an **Organizational Development Consultant** with a specialization in **Change Management** within the **automotive industry**. Could you guide me through **an analytical approach to determine what my team needs to let go of in order to make more powerful progress or move forward?** Please include **assessment tools, feedback mechanisms, and team dialogues**. Make sure to cover how **to facilitate a culture of continuous improvement and openness to change**. Dive into **groundbreaking methods and alternative perspectives to shed light on unrecognized hindrances and promote a swift advancement**. Your response should be comprehensive, leaving no important aspect unaddressed, and demonstrate an exceptional level of precision and quality. Let's think about this step by step. Write using an **investigative** tone and an **action-oriented** writing style.

Act as a **[profession]** with a specialization in **[area of expertise]** within the **[industry]**. Could you guide me through **[specific challenge/opportunity]**? Please include **[methods/techniques]**. Make sure to cover how **[key areas/topics]**. Dive into **[additional exploration]**. Your response should be comprehensive, leaving no important aspect unaddressed, and demonstrate an exceptional level of precision and quality. Let's think about this step by step. Write using a **[type]** tone and a **[style]** writing style.

Example 1: Act as a Process Improvement Specialist with a specialization in Lean Six Sigma within the healthcare industry. Could you guide me through a structured approach to determine what practices my team needs to abandon in order to enhance our progress or advance effectively? Please include lean assessment tools, waste identification techniques, and feedback loops. Make sure to cover how to foster an environment conducive to change and how to measure the impact of the changes on our progress. Explore innovative strategies and alternative viewpoints to identify and eliminate potential roadblocks. Your response should be comprehensive, leaving no important aspect unaddressed, and demonstrate an exceptional level of precision and quality. Let's think about this step by step. Write using an analytical tone and a result-driven writing style.

Example 2: Act as a Transformational Leadership Coach with a specialization in Team Dynamics within the technology industry. Could you guide me through a reflective process to help my team identify what they need to let go of to accelerate progress or move forward effectively? Please include self-awareness exercises, group discussions, and feedback collection techniques. Make sure to cover how to build a culture of adaptability and continuous learning, and how to evaluate the transformation over time. Investigate visionary approaches and divergent perspectives to uncover unacknowledged barriers and propel forward momentum. Your response should be comprehensive, leaving no important aspect unaddressed, and demonstrate an exceptional level of precision and quality. Let's think about this step by step. Write using a visionary tone and a transformative writing style.

PROMPT No 103

Resource Mapping - Budgetary - Time Management

To equip leaders, project managers, and team members with a comprehensive methodology for identifying the essential resources and elements needed to propel a project or team forward, thereby ensuring timely and effective execution.

Act as a **Project Management Expert** with a specialization in **resource allocation** in the **aerospace industry**. Could you guide me through a **systematic approach to determine the resources or elements necessary to effectively advance a project or team**? Please include **resource mapping techniques, budgetary considerations, and time management strategies**. Make sure to cover how **to prioritize these resources based on project milestones and team capabilities**. Investigate unconventional optimization methods and innovative **resource management** solutions to **maximize efficiency**. Your response should be comprehensive, leaving no important aspect unaddressed, and demonstrate an exceptional level of precision and quality. Let's think about this step by step. Write using a **methodical** tone and a **professional writing** style.

Act as a **[profession]** with a specialization in **[area of expertise]** in the **[industry]**. Could you guide me through **[specific challenge/opportunity]**? Please include **[methods/techniques]**. Make sure to cover how **[key areas/topics]**. Investigate unconventional optimization methods and innovative **[area for innovation]** solutions to **[desired outcome]**. Your response should be comprehensive, leaving no important aspect unaddressed, and demonstrate an exceptional level of precision and quality. Let's think about this step by step. Write using a **[type]** tone and **[style]** writing style.

Example 1: Act as an Operations Manager with a specialization in lean management in the automotive industry. Could you guide me through a structured approach to identify the resources needed to streamline our manufacturing process? Please include inventory control methods, workforce optimization, and technology assessments. Make sure to cover how to align these resources with production goals and quality standards. Explore the use of AI and machine learning to enhance resource allocation. Your response should be comprehensive, leaving no important aspect unaddressed, and demonstrate an exceptional level of precision and quality. Let's think about this step by step. Write using an analytical tone and a process optimization style.

Example 2: Act as a Human Resources Consultant with a specialization in talent management in the tech industry. Could you guide me through a plan to determine the human and material resources necessary to scale our software development team? Please include talent acquisition strategies, training programs, and workspace considerations. Make sure to cover how to match these resources with project requirements and team growth objectives. Delve into remote work solutions and upskilling programs to maximize talent utility. Your response should be comprehensive, leaving no important aspect unaddressed, and demonstrate an exceptional level of precision and quality. Let's think about this step by step. Write using a strategic tone and a talent development style.

PROMPT No 104

Tags

Relational-Values - Informative - Culture-Enhancement

Goal

To furnish leaders with an insightful framework to discern the values that underline their team's interactions with each other and external stakeholders like clients. This will serve as the foundation for refining team dynamics, enhancing client relationships, and improving overall work culture.

Prompt

As an **Organizational Development Specialist** with specialization in **relational values** for the **financial sector**, could you guide me through **the process of uncovering the values that guide my team in establishing and sustaining productive relationships with colleagues and clients?** Include **techniques for qualitative and quantitative data gathering, types of questions to ask for self and peer assessments, and strategies to embed these values into organizational culture.** Make sure the guide covers **methods to tie these values to key performance indicators and client satisfaction metrics.** Introduce unique angles and future-proof applications. Let's think about this step by step. Write using an informative tone and factual writing style.

Formula

As a **[profession]** with specialization in **[focus area]** for the **[industry]**, could you guide me through **[contextual challenge/opportunity]**? Include **[methods/techniques]**. Make sure the guide covers **[tools/frameworks]**. Introduce unique angles and future-proof applications. Let's think about this step by step. Write using a **[type]** tone and **[style]** writing style.

Examples

Example 1: As a Human Resources Consultant with a focus on workplace culture in the nonprofit sector, could you assist me in discerning the values that drive my team's interactions with each other and our donors? Include survey methods, types of reflective exercises, and frameworks to help define these values clearly. Make sure the guide incorporates how these values can be included in donor engagement strategies. Offer unique angles like the ethical considerations in nonprofit work. Let's dissect this carefully. Write using a compassionate tone and a human-centric writing style.

Example 2: As a Business Coach specializing in team dynamics for the retail industry, could you guide me in identifying the values that shape my team's relationships with co-workers and customers? Include observation techniques, examples of open-ended questions for team discussions, and action plans for ongoing value reinforcement. Make sure the guide suggests how to link these values to customer satisfaction and retention metrics. Discuss unique angles such as the impact of consumer psychology on value formation. Let's break this down methodically. Write using a commercial tone and a practical writing style.

VALUES

PROMPT No 105

Tags

Exploration - Alignment - Integration

Goal

To explore and articulate a set of guiding values within a team that resonates with its members, fostering a conducive environment for their holistic development and realization of their potential, while aligning with the overarching organizational ethos.

Prompt

As a **Values Exploration Facilitator** specializing in **Team Development** within the **technology industry**. How can I meticulously **explore** and **articulate values** that could serve as **guiding principles** for my team, aiding them in **their journey towards realizing their potential**? Please provide a comprehensive **exploration process inclusive of engaging dialogues, reflective exercises, and validation mechanisms**, aimed at **uncovering values that resonate with the team while aligning with the broader organizational ethos**. Your discourse should delve into **fostering an open, reflective environment**, ensuring the **practical applicability of these values**, and methodologies for **integrating these values into daily operations and long-term development plans**. The discourse should be thorough, capturing all critical facets, and exemplifying a high level of precision and quality.

Formula

As a **[Profession]** specializing in **[Specialization]** within the **[Industry]**. How can I meticulously **[Primary Action]** and **[Secondary Action]** that could serve as **[Objective]** for my team, aiding them in **[Desired Outcome]**? Please provide a comprehensive **[Process/Methodology]** inclusive of **[Techniques]**, aimed at **[Specific Goal]**. Your discourse should delve into **[Key Areas of Focus]**, ensuring the **[Relevant Aspect]**, and methodologies for **[Integration/Application]**. The discourse should be thorough, capturing all critical facets, and exemplifying a high level of precision and quality.

Example 1: As a Guiding Principles Analyst specializing in Team Cohesion within the finance sector. How can I meticulously explore and articulate values that could serve as guiding principles for my team, aiding them in their journey towards realizing their potential? Please provide a comprehensive exploration process inclusive of interactive discussions, self-assessment exercises, and validation surveys, aimed at discovering values that resonate with the team while aligning with the broader organizational ethos. Your discourse should delve into fostering a collaborative, reflective environment, ensuring the tangible applicability of these values, and methodologies for embedding these values into daily interactions and strategic planning. The discourse should be thorough, capturing all critical facets, and exemplifying a high level of precision and quality.

Example 2: As a Values Discovery Coordinator specializing in Employee Growth within the automotive sector. How can I meticulously explore and articulate values that could serve as guiding principles for my team, aiding them in their journey towards realizing their potential? Please provide a comprehensive exploration process inclusive of open forums, reflective journaling, and peer validation, aimed at unearthing values that resonate with the team while aligning with the broader organizational ethos. Your discourse should delve into fostering an inclusive, reflective environment, ensuring the actionable applicability of these values, and methodologies for assimilating these values into daily workflows and career development initiatives. The discourse should be thorough, capturing all critical facets, and exemplifying a high level of precision and quality.

PROMPT No 106

Articulation - Cohesion - Engagement

To delineate a methodical process for elucidating and articulating the values inherent within a team, with the aim of fostering a cohesive and value-driven team dynamic, which in turn, augments collective performance and job satisfaction.

Act as an **Organizational Culture Strategist** with a specialization in **Value Articulation** within the **healthcare sector**. Could you guide me through a **meticulous process to clarify and articulate the values of my team in a manner that augments team cohesion and enhances the collective ethos**? Please include **value-discovery workshops, stakeholder engagement, and communication strategies.** Make sure to cover how to **foster a conducive environment for open dialogue, utilize collaborative platforms for value articulation, and ensure the alignment of team values with organizational objectives.** Explore **innovative methodologies to ensure the values are well-understood, embraced, and enacted upon by all team members.** Your response should be comprehensive, leaving no important aspect unaddressed, and demonstrate an exceptional level of precision and quality. Let's think about this step by step. Write using an **engaging** tone and a **methodical** writing style.

Act as a [profession] with a specialization in [area of expertise] within the [industry]. Could you guide me through [specific challenge/opportunity]? Please include [methods/techniques]. Make sure to cover how [key areas/topics]. Explore [additional exploration]. Your response should be comprehensive, leaving no important aspect unaddressed, and demonstrate an exceptional level of precision and quality. Let's think about this step by step. Write using a [type] tone and a [style] writing style.

Example 1: Act as a Team Development Consultant with a specialization in Value Communication within the automotive industry. Could you guide me through a structured approach to clarify and articulate the values of my team, ensuring they serve as a robust foundation for collective action and decision-making? Please include value identification sessions, collaborative value articulation exercises, and internal communication plans. Make sure to cover how to create an atmosphere of trust, utilize digital platforms for ongoing value discussions, and align team values with broader organizational goals. Delve into novel approaches to ensure a vibrant value culture within the team. Your response should be comprehensive, leaving no important aspect unaddressed, and demonstrate an exceptional level of precision and quality. Let's think about this step by step. Write using a motivating tone and a solution-oriented writing style.

Example 2: Act as a Corporate Value Architect with a specialization in Value Integration within the technology sector. Could you guide me through a detailed process to elucidate and articulate the values of my team in a way that galvanizes a shared sense of purpose and enhances team synergy? Please include value clarification workshops, multi-level stakeholder engagement, and strategic communication channels. Make sure to cover how to establish a culture of open value expression, leverage interactive platforms for value articulation, and ensure the congruence of team values with organizational vision. Probe into forward-thinking methodologies to ensure the sustainable embodiment of articulated values in everyday team operations. Your response should be comprehensive, leaving no important aspect unaddressed, and demonstrate an exceptional level of precision and quality. Let's think about this step by step. Write using a visionary tone and a strategic writing style.

PROMPT No 107

Workshops - Principles - Resonance

To elucidate a systematic approach for identifying core values and guiding principles that can equip the team with insightful guidance to adeptly navigate through challenges, thereby fostering a resilient and value-driven team culture.

Act as an **Organizational Values Specialist** with a specialization in **Values Identification and Application** within the **manufacturing industry**. Could you guide me through **a meticulous process to identify the values and guiding principles that can provide insight and guidance to my team when** navigating challenges? Please include **value-discovery workshops, stakeholder consultations, and real-world application scenarios**. Make sure to cover how **to ensure the resonance of these values with team members, foster an understanding of the application of these principles in problem-solving, and measure the impact of value-driven decisions on team resilience and problem-solving efficacy.** Delve into **innovative and perhaps unconventional methodologies to ensure a deep-rooted understanding and adherence to these values.** Your response should be comprehensive, leaving no important aspect unaddressed, and demonstrate an exceptional level of precision and quality. Let's think about this step by step. Write using a **reflective** tone and a **structured** writing style.

Formula

Act as a **[profession]** with a specialization in **[area of expertise]** within the **[industry]**. Could you guide me through **[specific challenge/opportunity]**? Please include **[methods/techniques]**. Make sure to cover how **[key areas/topics]**. Delve into **[additional exploration]**. Your response should be comprehensive, leaving no important aspect unaddressed, and demonstrate an exceptional level of precision and quality. Let's think about this step by step. Write using a **[type]** tone and a **[style]** writing style.

Examples

Example 1: Act as a Corporate Ethicist with a specialization in Value-Driven Leadership within the financial sector. Could you guide me through a comprehensive process to unearth the values and guiding principles that could serve as a lighthouse for my team amidst challenges? Please include value-mapping exercises, ethical dilemma scenarios, and feedback loops. Make sure to cover how to align these values with organizational ethos, instill a value-centric mindset in team members, and assess the repercussions of value-based decisions on team morale and problem-solving capabilities. Probe into avant-garde methodologies to embed these values deeply within the team's modus operandi. Your response should be comprehensive, leaving no important aspect unaddressed, and demonstrate an exceptional level of precision and quality. Let's think about this step by step. Write using a probing tone and a methodical writing style.

Example 2: Act as a Values Integration Consultant with a specialization in Resilience Building within the education sector. Could you guide me through a nuanced approach to pinpoint the values and guiding principles that can enlighten and steer my team through adversities? Please include value-clarification sessions, ethical role-playing, and impact assessment techniques. Make sure to cover how to cultivate a shared understanding of these values, foster a culture of ethical reflection, and gauge the effectiveness of value-guided actions in overcoming challenges. Venture into pioneering and perhaps unorthodox approaches to ensure these values are deeply ingrained and acted upon. Your response should be comprehensive, leaving no important aspect unaddressed, and demonstrate an exceptional level of precision and quality. Let's think about this step by step. Write using an analytical tone and a detailed-oriented writing style.

Prioritization - Personal - Reflection

Goal

To provide a structured approach for individuals to establish the relative order of importance of their values, considering their priority in both personal and professional life. The aim is to facilitate better decision-making, enhance self-awareness, and improve alignment with life goals.

Prompt

As a **Values Alignment Specialist** in the **non-profit sector**, could you offer a **systematic methodology** to help **me** establish the relative order of importance of **my** values, considering their priority in **my life**? Include **actionable steps** for immediate application. Organize your insights into **thematic clusters**, each backed by **evidence from reputable journals**. Investigate **unexpected avenues and creative pathways**. Let's **scrutinize this topic incrementally**. Write using an **introspective** tone and a **reflective** writing style.

Formula

As a **[profession]** in the **[industry]**, could you offer a **[systematic methodology/comprehensive guide/structured framework]** to help **[me/us/them]** establish the relative order of importance of **[my/our/their]** values, considering their priority in **[my/our/their]** **[life/lives]**? Include **[actionable steps/practical solutions/immediate measures]** for **[immediate/short-term/long-term]** application. Organize your insights into **[thematic clusters/distinct categories/individual segments]**, each backed by **[evidence from/references from/data from]** **[reputable journals/credible research/authoritative publications]**. Investigate **[unexpected avenues/creative pathways/alternative perspectives]**. Let's **[scrutinize this topic incrementally/examine each dimension meticulously]**. Write using a **[introspective/reflective/contemplative]** tone and a **[reflective/nuanced/thoughtful]** writing style.

Examples

Example 1: As a Life Coach in the healthcare industry, could you offer a comprehensive guide to help me establish the relative order of importance of my values, considering their priority in my personal life? Include practical solutions for immediate application. Organize your insights into distinct categories, each backed by references from credible research. Investigate unexpected avenues and creative pathways. Let's examine each dimension meticulously. Write using a contemplative tone and a nuanced writing style.

Example 2: As a Leadership Consultant in the finance sector, could you offer a structured framework to help us establish the relative order of importance of our values, considering their priority in our professional lives? Include immediate measures for long-term application. Organize your insights into individual segments, each substantiated by data from authoritative publications. Investigate alternative perspectives and creative pathways. Let's scrutinize this topic incrementally. Write using an introspective tone and a thoughtful writing style.

PROMPT No 109

Tags

Weaknesses - Improvement - SelfAwareness

Goal

To gain practical strategies and approaches that will aid in facilitating my team's self-awareness and understanding of how their weaknesses might impact their work, ultimately supporting their professional growth and performance.

Prompt

As a **Leadership Development Consultant**, adopting a **constructive and empathetic tone**, could you outline the specific strategies and steps that I can employ to help **my team** assess and understand **the impact of their weaknesses on their work**? This is particularly relevant given the goal of **fostering self-awareness and continuous improvement within the team.**

Formula

As a **[profession]**, adopting a **[tone of voice]**, could you outline the specific strategies and steps that I can employ to help **[my/their]** **[team/group/department]** understand and assess **[contextual challenge/opportunity]**? This is particularly relevant given the goal of **[desired outcome]**.

Examples

Example 1: As a Team Coach, adopting an understanding and supportive tone, could you outline the specific strategies and steps that I can employ to help my sales team understand and assess the impact of their weaknesses on their sales performance? This is particularly relevant given the goal of fostering self-awareness and continuous improvement within the sales team.

Example 2: As a Talent Development Specialist, adopting a constructive and empathetic tone, could you outline the specific strategies and steps that a project manager can employ to help their project team understand and assess the impact of their weaknesses on the project outcomes? This is particularly relevant given the goal of fostering self-awareness and continuous improvement within the project team.

PROMPT No 110

Tags

Resilience - Anxiety - Strategies

Goal

To gain specific strategies or methods that a team can utilize to successfully overcome their fear and anxiety that stem from long-standing habits, fostering a more confident and resilient team.

Prompt

As a **Mental Health Consultant**, adopting a **compassionate and understanding tone**, could you provide specific strategies or methods that **my team** can utilize to successfully overcome **their fear and anxiety that stem from long-standing habits**? This is particularly relevant given the goal of **fostering a more confident and resilient team**.

As a **[profession]**, adopting a **[tone of voice]**, could you provide specific strategies or methods that **[my/their]** **[team/group/department]** can utilize to successfully overcome **[contextual challenge/opportunity]**? This is particularly relevant given the goal of **[desired outcome]**.

Example 1: As a Wellness Coach, adopting a supportive and empathetic tone, could you provide specific strategies or methods that my sales team can utilize to successfully overcome their fear and anxiety that stem from long-standing habits? This is particularly relevant given the goal of fostering a more confident and resilient sales team.

Example 2: As a Life Coach, adopting an encouraging and positive tone, could you provide specific strategies or methods that the marketing department can utilize to successfully overcome their fear and anxiety that stem from long-standing habits? This is particularly relevant given the goal of fostering a more confident and resilient marketing department.

PROMPT No 111

Weaknesses - Growth   - Team-Dynamics

To create a comprehensive strategy that equips business leaders with the tools and techniques to identify the genuine weaknesses within their teams. The end objective is to enhance productivity, teamwork, and professional development for each team member.

As a **Leadership Development Coach** specializing in **team dynamics** for the **tech startup sector**, could you guide me through the **process of uncovering the real weaknesses within my team**? Additionally, can you help me outline an action plan **to turn these weaknesses into opportunities for growth**? Please provide guidance on **initiating the conversation, the types of questions to ask that elicit truthful responses, techniques** for **creating an open and non-threatening environment, and how to proceed after identifying the weaknesses to formulate actionable plans for improvement.** Include elements that emphasize **the importance of self-assessment, peer-to-peer feedback, and measurable outcomes**. Introduce unique angles and prophetic opportunities. Let's think about this step by step. Write using an informative tone and factual writing style.

As a **[profession]** specializing in **[topic/specialization]** for the **[industry]**, could you guide me through the process of **[contextual challenge/opportunity]**? Additionally, can you help me outline an action plan to **[specific goal]**? Please provide guidance on **[methods/techniques/steps]** for **[specific aspects]**. Include elements that emphasize **[aspects/topics to be covered]**. Introduce unique angles and prophetic opportunities. Let's think about this step by step. Write using an **[tone]** and **[writing style]**.

Example 1: As a Corporate Culture Expert specializing in emotional intelligence for the finance industry, could you guide me through the process of identifying the actual emotional and interpersonal weaknesses within my team? Additionally, can you help me draft a strategy to uplift these skills? Please provide icebreakers for initiating the conversation, and methods for eliciting honest feedback. Include elements like EQ assessments and encourage a focus on both individual and collective emotional growth. Introduce breakthrough techniques and foresighted opportunities. Let's analyze this piece by piece. Write using a friendly tone and approachable writing style.

Example 2: As a Talent Development Specialist with a focus on technical skills in the healthcare sector, could you guide me through the method of recognizing the practical and technical weaknesses affecting my team? Additionally, can you assist me in crafting an actionable improvement plan? Please include methods for quantitatively assessing skill levels and approaches for soliciting direct feedback from peers and supervisors. Ensure the guide elaborates on how to utilize performance metrics for a data-driven analysis. Introduce pioneering approaches and futuristic solutions. Let's dissect this carefully. Write using an analytical tone and systematic writing style.

Final Words

In the domain of coaching, mentoring, and leadership, navigating the complexities requires a disciplined approach. This book aims to be an instrumental guide, leveraging artificial intelligence and prompt engineering to provide actionable insights for those in any profession. I have presented a curated list of prompts, each serving a specific objective: to clarify roles, define leadership strategies, and optimize coaching techniques, to name a few.

The scope of this book goes beyond a mere compilation of prompts. My goal is to impart a strategic mindset for interpreting challenges as opportunities, seeing barriers as milestones for growth, and viewing the future as a dynamic environment that can be strategically managed.

For the reader who began with skepticism, I hope you conclude this book with a newfound confidence, equipped with a toolkit that elevates your professional standing. For the experienced practitioner, may the methods and strategies here serve to refine your existing approaches.

This journey, while individual in nature, is set against the backdrop of collective human experience. Artificial intelligence serves as a bridge to this collective wisdom, streamlining the path toward your professional and personal development objectives.

In summary, this book aims to leave you not just prepared but empowered. As you close this chapter and move forward in your career, be reminded that each decision and action point offers an opportunity for growth and leadership. This is not just preparation; it is empowerment for transformative impact.

The challenges you face should be viewed as opportunities for demonstrating your leadership and expertise. I encourage you to approach these with a strategic focus, grounded in the knowledge and insights you have gained from this book.

I wish you all the best.

Mauricio

PS: Enjoyed your book? Scan the QR code to quickly leave a review where you purchased it. Your feedback is invaluable!

Appendix No 1

Sign-In to Chatbots

1.1. Chat GPT

Step 1: Visit ChatGPT on https://chat.openai.com/chat Click on "Sign Up" and then create your account.

Step 2: Verify your Account. You'd have to enter your details, verify your email and give an OTP you'll receive on your phone.

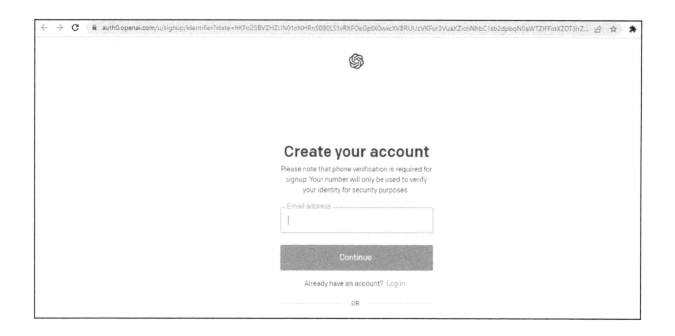

Once done, you'd have access to the free version of ChatGPT

As of April 2023, ChatGPT 3.5 is free to use and ChatGPT-4 costs $20 per month. As a beginner, you can easily test your skills on the free version.

This is how it looks:

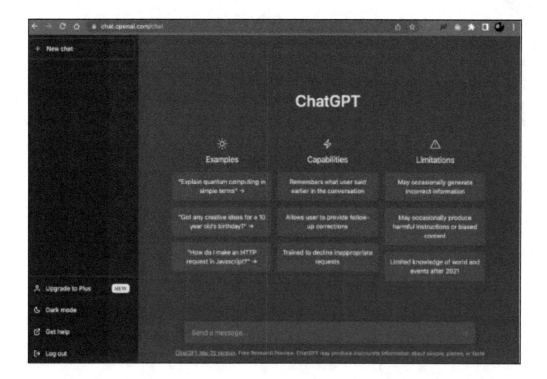

At the very bottom is where you'd chat:

You can now ask GPT anything you want, and it'll give you the desired result

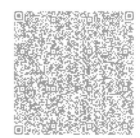

Note: The procedure outlined was developed based on the instructions available at the time of writing. If you require further assistance with signing up for ChatGPT, please scan this QR code:

1.2. Bing Chat

Step 1: Go to the Microsoft website (www.microsoft.com).

Locate the download page for Edge or look for "Microsoft Edge" in the search bar. If you don't want to download Microsoft Edge, go directly to Step 6. For better results, we recommend using Microsoft Edge.

Step 2: Click the download button and choose the version that fits your system.

Step 3: Once downloaded, open the setup file.

Step 4: A User Account Control dialog box will appear – click "Yes" to grant permission.

The installation wizard will guide you through a series of prompts and options. Review them carefully.

Step 5: To open Microsfot Edge, press Win + R on the keyboard to open the Run window.
In the Open field, type "microsoft-edge:" and press Enter on the keyboard or click or tap OK. Microsoft Edge is now open.

Step 6: Head to bing.com/chat

Step 7: From the pop-up that appears, click 'Start chatting'

Step 8: Enter the email address for the Microsoft account you'd like to use and click 'Next'.

If you don't have one, click 'Create one!' just under the text box and follow the instructions. Enter your password when prompted and click Next. From the following screen, choose whether you'd like to stay signed in or not. Click 'Chat Now'

Step 9: Choose your conversation style. If you've never used it before, it's best to stick with 'More Balanced'

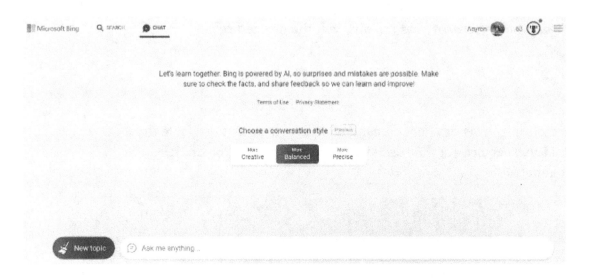

That's it! You can now start chatting.

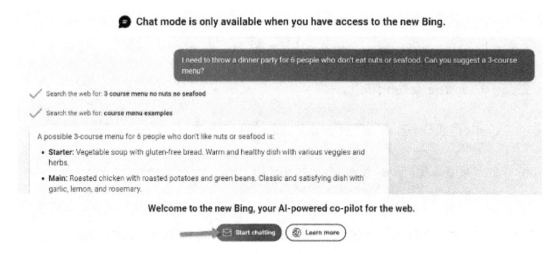

<u>**Note:**</u> The procedure outlined was developed based on the instructions available at the time of writing. If you require assistance with signing up for Bing Chat, please scan this QR code:

1.3. Google Bard

Step 1: Go to bard.google.com. Select Try Bard. Accept Google Bard Terms of Service

Step 2: Go to "Sign in"

Step 3: Enter a query or search term and then hit enter.

Wait for the AI to respond. You can then either continue the conversation or select Google It to use the traditional search engine.

Note: The procedure outlined was developed based on the instructions available at the time of writing. If you require assistance with signing up for Google Bard, please scan this QR code:

1.4. Meta LLaMA

Getting the Models

Step 1: Go to https://ai.meta.com/resources/models-and-libraries/llama-downloads/

Step 2: Fill the form with your information.

Step 3: Accept their license (if you agree with it)

Step 4: Once your request is approved, you will receive a signed URL over email.

Step 5: Clone the Llama 2 repository (go to https://github.com/facebookresearch/llama).

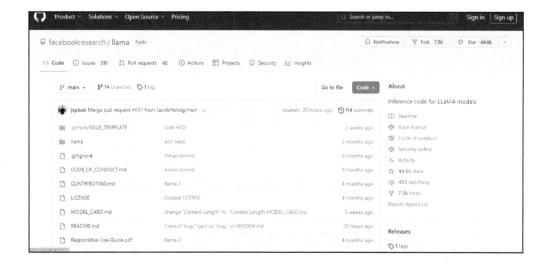

Step 6: Run the download.sh script, passing the URL provided when prompted to start the download. Keep in mind that the links expire after 24 hours and a certain amount of downloads. If you start seeing errors such as 403: Forbidden, you can always re-request a link.

Appendix No 2

Follow-up Prompts

There are 1100 prompts that you can use as follow-ups in order to get more specific or revised information from ChatGPT and other Chatbots. Don't forget to tailor these prompts to your specific circumstances and to the response you previously received from the Chatbot.

Each of these prompt types serves a different purpose and can be used effectively in different scenarios. Depending on the context and the intended outcome, one type of prompt may be more suitable than another.

These prompts are divided into eleven distinct categories, each tailored to specific conversational needs: Generic, Enhancement, Clarification, Probing, Critical Thinking, Instructional, Exploration, Comparison, Summarization, Evaluation, and Hypothetical.

To have access to 1100 follow-up prompts, please scan this QR code:

Appendix No 3

A Beginner's Step-by-Step Guide to Using ChatGPT

If you're new to ChatGPT, don't fret. This guide is designed to walk you through its use, step by step. By the end, you'll have a solid grasp of how to harness the power of this incredible tool.

Step 1: Accessing the Platform

Visit OpenAI's Platform: Head to OpenAI's official website: ChatGPT [openai.com]

Sign Up/Log In: If you don't have an account, you'll need to sign up. If you already have one, simply log in.

Step 2: Navigating the Interface

Dashboard: This is your central hub, where you can access various tools and see your usage stats.

Start a New Session: To interact with ChatGPT, start a new session or use a predefined platform depending on the current interface.

Step 3: Interacting with ChatGPT

Input Field: This is where you'll type or paste the prompts from our book.

Submit: Once you've entered your prompt, press 'Enter' or click the 'Submit' button.

Review Output: ChatGPT will generate a response. Take a moment to read and understand it.

Step 4: Refining Your Interaction

Being Specific: If you need specific information or a particular type of response, make your prompts more detailed.

Iterate: If the first response isn't what you're looking for, tweak your prompt and try again.

Step 5: Utilizing the Prompts from This Book

Choose a Prompt: Browse the book's prompt section and select one that aligns with your current needs.

Input: Copy and paste or type the chosen prompt into ChatGPT's input field.

Customization: Feel free to adjust the prompts to be more specific to your situation.

Step 6: Safety and Best Practices

Sensitive Information: Never share sensitive personal information, such as Social Security numbers or bank details, with ChatGPT or any online platform.

Understanding Outputs: Remember, while ChatGPT can produce human-like responses, it doesn't understand context in the same way humans do. Always review its advice with a critical eye.

Step 7: Exploring Advanced Features

As you become more comfortable with ChatGPT:

Experiment: Play around with different types of prompts to see the diverse responses you can get.

Integrate with Other Tools: There are several third-party tools and platforms that have integrated ChatGPT. Explore these to maximize your work.

Step 8: Stay Updated

Technology, especially in the AI field, evolves rapidly. Periodically check OpenAI's official channels for updates, new features, or changes to the platform.

By following this guide, even the most tech-averse individuals will find themselves comfortably navigating and interacting with ChatGPT. As we delve deeper into the book and introduce specific prompts tailored for your work you'll be equipped with the knowledge to make the most of them.

Here is our "*Elevate Your Productivity Using ChatGPT*" Guide: To access this guide to boost your efficiency and productivity, please scan this QR code.

Appendix No 4

Mentoring, Coaching, and Leadership Professionals

This list encompasses professions pivotal in nurturing growth, leadership, and collaboration in work settings. They play crucial roles in guiding, training, and inspiring individuals towards achieving personal and organizational objectives.

1. Mentor: Provides guidance, support, and wisdom to less experienced individuals for personal and professional growth.
2. Coach: Assists in developing specific skills, improving performance, and achieving defined objectives through structured guidance.
3. Leader: Guides, inspires, and influences a group towards achieving common goals, fostering positive organizational culture.
4. Executive Coach: Assists executives in honing leadership skills, achieving goals, and navigating career transitions.
5. Life Coach: Guides individuals in personal development, goal-setting, and achieving life balance.
6. Career Counselor: Provides advice on career exploration, development strategies, and job search.
7. Organizational Consultant: Aids organizations in improving performance, culture, and change management.
8. Training and Development Manager: Plans, directs, and coordinates programs to enhance employee skills.
9. Human Resources Manager: Oversees recruitment, employee relations, and organizational development.
10. Management Consultant: Advises on business strategies, problem-solving, and organizational improvements.
11. Leadership Development Specialist: Creates programs to develop leadership capabilities within organizations.
12. Performance Coach: Helps individuals improve performance and achieve professional objectives.
13. Business Coach: Guides entrepreneurs in business growth, strategy, and problem-solving.
14. Conflict Resolution Specialist: Aids in resolving disputes and improving communication in workplaces.
15. Executive Search Consultant: Assists organizations in identifying and recruiting executive leadership talent.
16. Team Building Specialist: Designs and facilitates activities to enhance team cohesion.
17. Corporate Trainer: Provides training to improve employee skills and knowledge.
18. Sales Trainer: Develops and delivers training programs to improve sales team performance and effectiveness.
19. Communication Coach: Improves interpersonal communication skills within professional settings.
20. Industrial-Organizational Psychologist: Applies psychological principles to improve workplace dynamics.
21. Change Management Consultant: Guides organizations through change with strategies to ensure smooth transitions.
22. Culture Development Consultant: Aids in cultivating a positive, productive organizational culture.

23. Educational Consultant: Advises on educational strategies, curriculum development, and leadership.
24. Talent Development Specialist: Identifies and nurtures employee talents for organizational growth.
25. Learning and Development Specialist: Designs and implements training programs to promote employee growth and organizational success.
26. Supply Chain Manager: Oversees the end-to-end supply chain process to ensure efficiency and effectiveness.
27. Negotiation Consultant: Aids in enhancing negotiation skills and strategies.
28. Mediator: Facilitates resolution of disputes in a neutral manner.
29. Employee Engagement Consultant: Boosts employee satisfaction and productivity through engagement strategies.
30. Entrepreneurship Advisor: Guides individuals in launching and growing their own businesses.

Appendix No 5

Specializations for Mentors, Coaches and Leaders

1. This compilation presents specialized roles integral to fostering excellence, innovation, and resilience within professional landscapes, offering tailored guidance and support to propel individuals and businesses toward their aspirations.
2. Leadership: Enhancing skills for leading teams and organizations effectively.
3. Performance: Boosting individual or team productivity and output.
4. Career: Navigating career progression and transitions.
5. Sales: Increasing sales proficiency and results.
6. Marketing: Crafting and executing marketing strategies.
7. Strategy: Formulating and applying long-term business plans.
8. Innovation: Fostering creative thinking and new ideas.
9. Culture: Shaping positive organizational values and practices.
10. Conflict Resolution: Managing and resolving disputes effectively.
11. Communication Skills: Improving sharing and receiving of information.
12. Emotional Intelligence: Understanding and managing emotions for improved interactions.
13. Team Dynamics: Strengthening team cooperation and function.
14. Change Leadership: Guiding successful organizational change.
15. Diversity and Inclusion: Building respectful, diverse work environments.
16. Work-Life Balance: Balancing professional responsibilities with personal life.
17. Organizational Development: Enhancing organizational structures and efficiency.
18. Time Management: Prioritizing tasks and managing time wisely.
19. Customer Success: Ensuring clients achieve their desired outcomes.
20. Negotiation Skills: Reaching agreements effectively and advantageously.
21. Personal Branding: Crafting and communicating a personal image.
22. Corporate Governance: Directing company management and policies.
23. Business Ethics: Promoting ethical professional conduct.
24. Financial Coaching for Executives: Managing company finances and economic strategy.
25. Talent Development: Growing employee skills and career paths.
26. Digital Transformation: Integrating digital technology into all business areas.
27. Entrepreneurship: Starting and growing new business ventures.
28. Global Leadership: Leading across diverse cultures and markets.
29. Sustainability Leadership: Integrating eco-friendly practices into business.
30. Crisis Leadership: Leading effectively through emergencies.

Tones

Tone reflects the emotional stance towards the subject or audience, impacting engagement and receptivity. In coaching or leadership, the right tone fosters trust, motivation, and effective communication, aligning with growth-oriented goals.

1. Motivational: Inspiring action and positivity towards achieving goals.
2. Empathetic: Demonstrating understanding and compassion towards others' experiences.
3. Authoritative: Exuding confidence and expertise in guiding others.
4. Inspirational: Provoking thought and encouraging higher aspirations.
5. Supportive: Offering encouragement and backing during challenges.
6. Reflective: Encouraging contemplation and self-assessment.
7. Directive: Providing clear, actionable guidance.
8. Analytical: Examining situations critically and logically.
9. Advisory: Offering suggestions based on expertise.
10. Challenging: Encouraging stretching beyond comfort zones.
11. Respectful: Honoring individuals' values, thoughts, and feelings.
12. Humorous: Adding levity to engage and ease tension.
13. Socratic: Encouraging critical thinking through questioning.
14. Constructive: Providing feedback for growth and improvement.
15. Patient: Showing understanding and tolerance during learning processes.
16. Optimistic: Highlighting the positive and potential success.
17. Realistic: Providing a practical and sensible perspective.
18. Encouraging: Boosting morale and self-efficacy.
19. Appreciative: Acknowledging efforts and achievements.
20. Reassuring: Alleviating concerns and instilling confidence.
21. Inquisitive: Encouraging exploration and curiosity.
22. Observational: Noting and reflecting on behaviors and outcomes.
23. Persuasive: Convincing others towards a certain viewpoint.
24. Resilient: Demonstrating toughness and adaptability in adversity.
25. Visionary: Focusing on long-term potential and broader horizons.
26. Collegial: Promoting a sense of partnership and teamwork.
27. Energizing: Infusing enthusiasm and vigor.
28. Compassionate: Showing care and understanding in dealing with others.
29. Professional: Maintaining a formal and respectful demeanor.
30. Mindful: Demonstrating awareness and consideration.

Appendix No 7

Writing Styles

Writing style denotes how ideas are expressed, encompassing word choice and narrative flow. In coaching, mentoring, and leadership, an apt style clarifies concepts, provides guidance, and facilitates meaningful exploration of ideas.

1. Expository: Explaining facts and information clearly and straightforwardly.
2. Descriptive: Painting a vivid picture to convey a particular scenario or idea.
3. Narrative: Telling a story or recounting events to convey lessons or insights.
4. Persuasive: Arguing a point or encouraging a particular action or mindset.
5. Concise: Delivering information in a brief, direct manner.
6. Analytical: Dissecting information to understand and convey underlying principles.
7. Reflective: Encouraging introspection and consideration of past experiences.
8. Dialogic: Engaging in a two-way conversation to explore ideas.
9. Illustrative: Using examples and anecdotes to clarify points.
10. Instructive: Providing detailed guidance or instructions.
11. Interpretive: Explaining and making sense of complex concepts.
12. Comparative: Analyzing similarities and differences between concepts.
13. Argumentative: Making a case for a particular stance or action.
14. Problem-Solution: Identifying issues and proposing solutions.
15. Evaluative: Assessing the value or effectiveness of certain practices.
16. Journalistic: Reporting facts in an objective, straightforward manner.
17. Exploratory: Delving into topics to discover new insights or perspectives.
18. Contemplative: Encouraging deep thought on certain topics.
19. Case Study: Delving into real-world examples to extract lessons.
20. Research-based: Grounding discourse in empirical evidence.
21. Informal: Adopting a casual, accessible approach.
22. Formal: Adhering to professional language and structure.
23. Technical: Utilizing specialized terminology relevant to the field.
24. Conceptual: Exploring ideas at a high level.
25. Practical: Focusing on actionable advice and real-world application.
26. Empirical: Relying on observation and experience.
27. Theoretical: Delving into theories and abstract concepts.
28. Storyboard: Unfolding ideas through a sequenced narrative.
29. Interactive: Encouraging active engagement from the reader.
30. Scenario-based: Outlining hypothetical situations to explore concepts.

Appendix No 8

Tags

	Chapter	Tag 1	Tag 2	Tag 3
Prompt 1	Accountability	Accountability	Leadership	Performance
Prompt 2	Accountability	Team Accountability	Solution-Oriented	Professional Setting
Prompt 3	Accountability	Growth Cultivation	Fulfillment Fostering	Team Development
Prompt 4	Accountability	Management	Diversity	Strategies
Prompt 5	Accountability	Sustainability	Expenses	Debt Mitigation
Prompt 6	Awareness	Self-Awareness	Work Ethic	High-Performance Culture
Prompt 7	Awareness	Autonomous Assessment	Training Effectiveness	Work Enhancement
Prompt 8	Awareness	Mission Influence	Organizational Culture	Team Mindset
Prompt 9	Awareness	Cohesive Culture	Organizational Success	Mission Cultivation
Prompt 10	Awareness	Resilience	Virtue	Communication
Prompt 11	Awareness	Reflection	Growth	Learning
Prompt 12	Belief	Assessment	Workload	Balance
Prompt 13	Belief	Alignment	Work-Ethic	Productivity
Prompt 14	Belief	Improvement	Change	Mindset
Prompt 15	Belief	Communication	Losses	Commitment
Prompt 16	Belief	Beliefs	Progress	Work
Prompt 17	Belief	Evolution	Beliefs	Identification
Prompt 18	Challenge	Solutions	Proactivity	Challenges
Prompt 19	Challenge	Exploration	Diversity	Analysis
Prompt 20	Challenge	Development	Growth	Challenges
Prompt 21	Challenge	Adaptation	Transition	Techniques
Prompt 22	Challenge	Team-Leadership	Strategies	Professional-Development
Prompt 23	Challenge	Productive-Discussion	Impediment	Insight
Prompt 24	Change	Diplomacy	Communication	Team-Feedback
Prompt 25	Change	Skills-Assessment	Implementation	Team-Development
Prompt 26	Change	Development	Skills	Adaptability
Prompt 27	Commitment	Engagement	Productivity	Remote-Work
Prompt 28	Creativity	Collaboration	Innovation	Originality
Prompt 29	Creativity	Productivity	Behavior	Performance
Prompt 30	Creativity	Creativity	Connection	Inspiration
Prompt 31	Decisions	Data-Driven	Accuracy	Integration
Prompt 32	Decisions	Leadership	Empowerment	Positivity
Prompt 33	Excitement	Virtual-Meetings	Creativity	Engagement
Prompt 34	Excitement	Efficiency	Precision	Time-Management
Prompt 35	Fear	Transparency	Empowerment	HR
Prompt 36	Fear	Motivation	Confidence	Leadership

Prompt 37	Feelings	Well-being	Productivity	Workplace
Prompt 38	Feelings	Self-Reflection	Emotions	Unconscious
Prompt 39	Feelings	Impact	Performance	Management
Prompt 40	Flow	Obstacles	Flow	Strategies
Prompt 41	Flow	Optimal-Self	Performance	Problem-Solving
Prompt 42	Fulfillment	Cohesion	Development	Realization
Prompt 43	Goals	Values	Integration	Aspirations
Prompt 44	Goals	Empowerment	Leadership	Strategies
Prompt 45	Goals	Resources	Development	Support
Prompt 46	Goals	Self-Improvement	Career	Conflict
Prompt 47	Habits	Quality	Efficiency	Error-Reduction
Prompt 48	Habits	Productivity	SocialMedia	Distractions
Prompt 49	Learning	Reflection	Growth	Improvement
Prompt 50	Learning	Improvement	Recognition	Learning
Prompt 51	Learning	Growth	Criteria	Evaluation
Prompt 52	Learning	Leadership	Wellbeing	Collaboration
Prompt 53	Learning	CriticalReview	Solutions	ActionableInsights
Prompt 54	Learning	Preparation	Conversation	Learning
Prompt 55	Learning	Reflection	Improvement	Strategy
Prompt 56	Listenning	Project-Management	Strategy	Progress
Prompt 57	Listenning	Public-Speaking	Professional-Development	Confidence
Prompt 58	Mindset	Operational	Efficiency	Barriers
Prompt 59	Mindset	Comfort	Productivity	Workplace
Prompt 60	Mindset	Communication	Leadership	Retention
Prompt 61	Mindset	Alignment	Goal-Setting	Entertainment
Prompt 62	Mindset	Resilience	Coping	Oil-and-Gas
Prompt 63	Options	Decision-Making	Development	Strategy
Prompt 64	Options	Risk-Mitigation	Opportunity-Leverage	Analysis
Prompt 65	Options	Leadership	Improvement	Finance
Prompt 66	Performance	Outcomes	Alignment	Clarity
Prompt 67	Performance	Goals	Prioritization	Repercussions
Prompt 68	Performance	Leadership	Collaboration	OrganizationalCulture
Prompt 69	Preferences	Prioritization	Facilitation	Reflection
Prompt 70	Priorities	PositiveCulture	Communication	Team-building
Prompt 71	Progress	Learning	Development	Professionalism
Prompt 72	Progress	Performance	Measurement	Team
Prompt 73	Purpose	Self-awareness	Career Trajectory	Introspection
Prompt 74	Purpose	Framework	Articulation	Collaboration
Prompt 75	Purpose	Decision-Making	Communication	Articulation
Prompt 76	Purpose	Self-Awareness	Media	Purpose
Prompt 77	Relationships	Roles	Construction	Allocation
Prompt 78	Relationships	Relationships	Communication	Collaboration

Prompt 79	Relationships	Presence	Engagement	Communication
Prompt 80	Relationships	Engagement	Persuasive	Organization
Prompt 81	Relationships	Communication	Conflict-Resolution	Construction
Prompt 82	Relationships	Alignment	Frameworks	Values
Prompt 83	Relationships	Resourcefulness	Mindset	Adaptability
Prompt 84	Relationships	Emotional-Intelligence	Cohesive	Resilience
Prompt 85	Relationships	Engagement	Productivity	Mindfulness
Prompt 86	Relationships	Resource Management	Utilization	Analytical Guide
Prompt 87	Self-assessment	Presentation	Development	Consulting
Prompt 88	Self-assessment	Accountability	Success	Analysis
Prompt 89	Self-assessment	Data	Collaboration	Continuous-improvement
Prompt 90	Skills	Motivation	Skills	Optimization
Prompt 91	Skills	Leadership	Feedback	Development
Prompt 92	Strategies	Innovation	Experimentation	Creativity
Prompt 93	Strength	Top-strengths	Progress	Motivation
Prompt 94	Strength	Scrutinizing	Strengths	Patterns
Prompt 95	Strength	Growth	Strengths	Development
Prompt 96	Strength	Evaluation	Strengths	Allocation
Prompt 97	Strength	Overleveraging	Performance	Adaptation
Prompt 98	Strength	Rejuvenation	Alignment	Assessment
Prompt 99	Strength	Ideation	Implementation	Engagement
Prompt 100	Support	Focus	Alignment	Productivity
Prompt 101	Support	Hindrances	Progression	Feedback
Prompt 102	Support	Resource Mapping	Budgetary	Time Management
Prompt 103	Support	Relational-Values	Informative	Culture-Enhancement
Prompt 104	Values	Exploration	Alignment	Integration
Prompt 105	Values	Articulation	Cohesion	Engagement
Prompt 106	Values	Workshops	Principles	Resonance
Prompt 107	Values	Prioritization	Personal	Reflection
Prompt 108	Weakness	Weaknesses	Improvement	SelfAwareness
Prompt 109	Weakness	Resilience	Anxiety	Strategies
Prompt 110	Weakness	Weaknesses	Growth	Team-Dynamics
Prompt 111	Weakness	Authenticity	Strengths	Downplaying

Appendix No 9

Unlock the Full Potential of This Book - Instantly

Dive into a world of convenience with our electronic copy! Feel free to seamlessly copy and paste any prompt that sparks your interest.

Customize them to fit your unique needs. Say goodbye to the hassle of retyping. Start crafting your perfect prompts with ease and efficiency!.

To access to the electronic copy, please scan this QR code:

www.ingramcontent.com/pod-product-compliance
Lightning Source LLC
LaVergne TN
LVHW082036050326
832904LV00005B/198